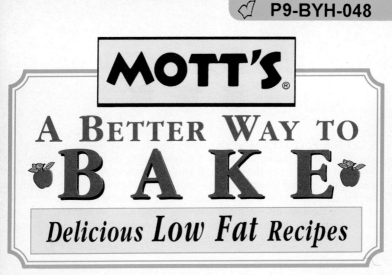

MOTT'S®

A BETTER WAY TO
❦ B A K E ❦

Delicious *Low Fat* Recipes

Introduction   2
Discover how to bake it healthy with apple sauce

Muffin Magic   4
Sound the wake-up call with these quick-to-fix, low fat recipes

Breakfast Delights   12
A delicious array of slimmed-down quick and yeast breads

Featherweight Cakes   32
Sensational ways to celebrate without overindulging

Tempting Treats   52
Scrumptious cookies and bars that satisfy any snack attack

Fit Finales   68
Lighter versions of your favorite desserts from tarts to tortes

Savory Creations   86
Tantalizing entrées and side dishes for health-minded meals

Index   94

INTRODUCTION

A BETTER WAY TO BAKE: Like many people today, you're probably concerned about the way you eat. Today's healthy diet means cutting down on fat, not just calories. Yet, if you're like most Americans, you still want to enjoy your favorite foods—especially delicious desserts—without sacrificing taste. Is there a way to achieve a balance between the delicious, satisfying food we love and our concerns about calories and fat? It seemed to be an unsolvable problem, until Mott's came along with a whole new idea that lets you "have your cake, and eat it, too!"

MOTT'S MAKES IT HEALTHIER: Fats typically provide the moisture and texture that make foods taste good. But now, Mott's has a better idea. Mott's Apple Sauce makes an excellent fat substitute in many recipes. It creates the desired moisture and texture with *no fat, no cholesterol* and only *a fraction of the calories.*

Now you can prepare tantalizing low fat versions of your favorite moist and rich-tasting banana bread, luscious fruit-filled muffins or that mouthwatering chocolate cake your family adores—all without guilt! Even entrée and side-dish recipes benefit from replacing fat with apple sauce.

Mott's makes it easy to indulge in luscious low fat recipes—no special baking or cooking techniques are required. You can use standard methods and familiar recipes for great-tasting, great-looking meals, desserts and treats.

A HEALTHIER WAY TO EAT: Mott's Apple Sauce is the smartest way to eat healthier because it has the wholesome goodness of real fruit with no fat, no cholesterol, no sodium and only 50 calories per four-ounce serving in Mott's Natural Apple Sauce. Just look at how much fat you can save by substituting one cup of Mott's Apple Sauce for one cup of butter, margarine, shortening or oil.

One Cup of:	Calories	Fat (grams)
Mott's Natural Apple Sauce	**100**	**0**
Butter or Margarine	1,625	184
Shortening	1,760	205
Oil	1,927	218

BREAK THE FAT BARRIER: Mott's Banana Bread uses one-half cup of Mott's Natural Apple Sauce instead of oil. This easy substitution reduces the fat usually found in a standard homemade loaf of banana bread by 109 grams and saves 964 calories.

If you're a packaged-mix baker, consider this: One-third cup of Mott's Natural Apple Sauce added to a store-bought yellow cake mix in place of oil saves 73 grams of fat and 642 calories. That's a lot less fat and calories for you and your family without any extra baking effort or any sacrifice of taste. Try substituting Mott's for fat in some of your favorite packaged mixes for cakes, breads and muffins. It's so simple—just replace the amount of oil or margarine listed on the package with the same amount of apple sauce.

FAT (grams)

NUTRITIONAL ANALYSIS: Every recipe in this cookbook is followed by a nutritional analysis that lists certain nutrient values for a single serving. The analysis of each recipe includes all the ingredients that are listed in that recipe, *except* ingredients listed as "optional" or "for garnish." If a range is offered for an ingredient ("¼ to ⅛ teaspoon" for example), the *first* amount given was used to calculate the nutrition information. If an ingredient is presented with an option ("½ cup blueberries or raspberries" for example), the *first* item listed was used to calculate the nutrition information. Foods shown in photographs on the same serving plate and offered as "serve with" or "garnish with" suggestions at the end of the recipe are *not* included in the nutritional analysis unless they are listed in the ingredient list. Unless otherwise specified, when using frozen fruit, be sure to purchase unsweetened fruit. If you do purchase sweetened frozen fruit, the fat content of the recipe will not change, but the extra sugar will increase the calorie count. Every effort has been made to give accurate nutritional data. However, because numerous variables account for a wide range of values for certain foods, all nutrient values that appear in this publication should be considered approximate.

TIPS: Any of these recipes can be prepared using a liquid egg substitute. Just replace each whole egg with ¼ cup of the substitute. There is no need to replace egg whites since the cholesterol is in the egg yolk, not the white.

Some of the recipes in this cookbook call for nonfat buttermilk. Sour milk can also be used. To sour milk, combine 1 tablespoon white vinegar plus enough skim milk to equal 1 cup. Stir; wait five minutes before using.

MUFFIN MAGIC

Peach Gingerbread Muffins

2 cups all-purpose flour
2 teaspoons baking powder
1 teaspoon ground ginger
½ teaspoon salt
½ teaspoon ground cinnamon
¼ teaspoon ground cloves
½ cup sugar
½ cup Mott's Chunky Apple
   Sauce

¼ cup Mott's Apple Juice
¼ cup Grandma's Molasses
1 egg
2 tablespoons vegetable oil
1 (16-ounce) can peaches in
   juice, drained and chopped

1. Preheat oven to 400°F. Line 12 (2½-inch) muffin cups with paper liners or spray with nonstick cooking spray.

2. In large bowl, combine flour, baking powder, ginger, salt and spices.

3. In small bowl, combine sugar, apple sauce, apple juice, molasses, egg and oil.

4. Stir apple sauce mixture into flour mixture just until moistened. Fold in peaches.

5. Spoon evenly into prepared muffin cups.

6. Bake 20 minutes or until toothpick inserted in center comes out clean. Immediately remove from pan; cool on wire rack 10 minutes. Serve warm or cool completely.   *Makes 12 servings*

Nutrients Per Serving:			
Calories	190	Sodium	150 mg
Total Fat	3.0 g	Cholesterol	20 mg
% of Calories From Fat	13		

Peach Gingerbread Muffins

Apple Bran Muffins

1½ cups all-purpose flour
2 teaspoons baking powder
1 teaspoon baking soda
½ teaspoon salt
¼ teaspoon ground nutmeg
½ cup sugar
2 tablespoons margarine,
softened

1½ cups Mott's Cinnamon Apple
Sauce
2 egg whites
2 tablespoons Grandma's
Molasses
1½ cups wheat bran flakes cereal

1. Preheat oven to 350°F. Line 12 (2½-inch) muffin cups with paper liners or spray with nonstick cooking spray.

2. In large bowl, combine flour, baking powder, baking soda, salt and nutmeg.

3. In medium bowl, beat sugar and margarine with electric mixer at medium speed until blended. Whisk in apple sauce, egg whites and molasses. Add cereal; stir until moistened.

4. Stir apple sauce mixture into flour mixture just until moistened.

5. Spoon evenly into prepared muffin cups.

6. Bake 25 to 30 minutes or until toothpick inserted in center comes out clean. Immediately remove from pan; cool on wire rack 10 minutes. Serve warm or cool completely.

Makes 12 servings

Nutrients Per Serving:			
Calories	160	Sodium	280 mg
Total Fat	2.0 g	Cholesterol	0 mg
% of Calories From Fat	12		

Banana Graham Muffins

2 cups graham cracker crumbs
1¾ cups all-purpose flour
⅓ cup firmly packed light brown sugar
1 tablespoon baking powder
½ teaspoon salt
2 ripe medium bananas, mashed (1 cup)

½ cup Mott's Natural Apple Sauce
¼ cup skim milk
1 egg
½ teaspoon vanilla extract
½ cup chopped pecans (optional)

1. Preheat oven to 400°F. Line 16 (2½-inch) muffin cups with paper liners or spray with nonstick cooking spray.

2. In large bowl, combine graham cracker crumbs, flour, brown sugar, baking powder and salt.

3. In medium bowl, whisk together bananas, apple sauce, milk, egg and vanilla.

4. Stir apple sauce mixture into flour mixture just until moistened. Fold in pecans, if desired.

5. Spoon evenly into prepared muffin cups.

6. Bake 20 to 25 minutes or until toothpick inserted in center comes out clean. Immediately remove from pan; cool on wire rack 10 minutes. Serve warm or cool completely.   *Makes 16 servings*

Nutrients Per Serving:			
Calories	130	Sodium	200 mg
Total Fat	1.5 g	Cholesterol	15 mg
% of Calories From Fat	10		

Blueberry Muffins

1 cup fresh or thawed, frozen
blueberries
1¾ cups plus 1 tablespoon
all-purpose flour, divided
2 teaspoons baking powder
1 teaspoon grated lemon peel
½ teaspoon salt

½ cup Mott's Apple Sauce
½ cup sugar
1 whole egg
1 egg white
2 tablespoons vegetable oil
¼ cup skim milk

1. Preheat oven to 375°F. Line 12 (2½-inch) muffin cups with paper liners or spray with nonstick cooking spray.

2. In small bowl, toss blueberries with 1 tablespoon flour.

3. In large bowl, combine remaining 1¾ cups flour, baking powder, lemon peel and salt.

4. In another small bowl, combine apple sauce, sugar, whole egg, egg white and oil.

5. Stir apple sauce mixture into flour mixture alternately with milk. Mix just until moistened. Fold in blueberry mixture.

6. Spoon evenly into prepared muffin cups.

7. Bake 20 minutes or until toothpick inserted in center comes out clean. Immediately remove from pan; cool on wire rack 10 minutes. Serve warm or cool completely.   *Makes 12 servings*

Nutrients Per Serving:			
Calories	150	Sodium	150 mg
Total Fat	3.0 g	Cholesterol	20 mg
% of Calories From Fat	18		

Blueberry Muffins

Heavenly Lemon Muffins

1 (16-ounce) package 1-step
    angel food cake mix
3 cups all-purpose flour
4 teaspoons baking powder
½ teaspoon salt
1 cup granulated sugar
⅔ cup skim milk
⅔ cup Mott's Natural Apple
    Sauce

¼ cup vegetable oil
2 egg whites
2 tablespoons grated lemon peel
2 teaspoons lemon extract
4 drops yellow food coloring
    (optional)
2 tablespoons powdered sugar
    (optional)

1. Preheat oven to 375°F. Line 24 (2½-inch) muffin cups with paper liners or spray with nonstick cooking spray.

2. In large bowl, prepare angel food cake mix according to package directions.

3. In another large bowl, combine flour, baking powder and salt.

4. In medium bowl, combine granulated sugar, milk, apple sauce, oil, egg whites, lemon peel, lemon extract and food coloring, if desired.

5. Stir apple sauce mixture into flour mixture just until moistened.

6. Fill each muffin cup ⅓ full with apple sauce batter. Top with angel food cake batter, filling each cup almost full.*

7. Bake 20 minutes or until golden and puffed. Immediately remove from pan; cool completely on wire rack. Sprinkle tops with powdered sugar, if desired. *Makes 24 servings*

*There will be some angel food cake batter remaining.

Heavenly Strawberry Muffins: Substitute strawberry extract for lemon extract and red food coloring for yellow food coloring, if desired. Eliminate lemon peel.

Nutrients Per Serving:			
Calories	190	Sodium	140 mg
Total Fat	2.5 g	Cholesterol	0 mg
% of Calories From Fat	12		

Top to bottom: Heavenly Lemon Muffins, Heavenly Strawberry Muffin

BREAKFAST DELIGHTS

Apple Sauce Cinnamon Rolls

ROLLS

4 cups all-purpose flour, divided
1 package active dry yeast
1 cup Mott's Natural Apple Sauce, divided
½ cup skim milk

⅓ cup plus 2 tablespoons granulated sugar, divided
2 tablespoons margarine
½ teaspoon salt
1 egg, beaten lightly
2 teaspoons ground cinnamon

ICING

1 cup sifted powdered sugar
1 tablespoon skim milk

½ teaspoon vanilla extract

1. **To prepare Rolls,** in large bowl, combine 1½ cups flour and yeast. In small saucepan, combine ¾ cup apple sauce, ½ cup milk, 2 tablespoons granulated sugar, margarine and salt. Cook over medium heat, stirring frequently, until mixture reaches 120° to 130°F and margarine is almost melted (milk will appear curdled). Add to flour mixture along with egg. Beat with electric mixer on low speed 30 seconds, scraping bowl frequently. Beat on high speed 3 minutes. Stir in 2¼ cups flour until soft dough forms.

2. Turn out dough onto lightly floured surface; flatten slightly. Knead 3 to 5 minutes or until smooth and elastic, adding remaining ¼ cup flour to prevent sticking if necessary. Shape dough into ball; place in large bowl sprayed with nonstick cooking spray. Turn dough over so that top is greased. Cover with towel; let rise in warm place about 1 hour or until doubled in bulk.

3. Spray two 8- or 9-inch round baking pans with nonstick cooking spray.

continued on page 14

Apple Sauce Cinnamon Rolls

Apple Sauce Cinnamon Rolls, continued

4. Punch down dough; turn out onto lightly floured surface. Cover with towel; let rest 10 minutes. Roll out dough into 12-inch square. Spread remaining ¼ cup apple sauce over dough, to within ½ inch of edges. In small bowl, combine remaining ⅓ cup granulated sugar and cinnamon; sprinkle over apple sauce. Roll up dough jelly-roll style. Moisten edge with water; pinch to seal seam. Cut roll into 12 (1-inch) slices with sharp floured knife. Arrange 6 rolls ½ inch apart in each prepared pan. Cover with towel; let rise in warm place about 30 minutes or until nearly doubled in bulk.

5. Preheat oven to 375°F. Bake 20 to 25 minutes or until lightly browned. Cool on wire rack 5 minutes. Invert each pan onto serving plate.

6. **To prepare Icing,** in small bowl, combine powdered sugar, 1 tablespoon milk and vanilla until smooth. Drizzle over tops of rolls. Serve warm.

Makes 12 servings

Nutrients Per Serving:			
Calories	260	Sodium	100 mg
Total Fat	3.0 g	Cholesterol	25 mg
% of Calories From Fat	10		

Corn Bread

1 cup all-purpose flour
1 cup yellow cornmeal
¼ cup sugar
1 tablespoon baking powder
1 teaspoon salt

1 cup skim milk
4 egg whites
¼ cup Mott's Natural Apple
Sauce

1. Preheat oven to 400°F. Spray 8-inch square baking pan with nonstick cooking spray.

2. In large bowl, combine flour, cornmeal, sugar, baking powder and salt.

3. In small bowl, combine milk, egg whites and apple sauce.

4. Stir apple sauce mixture into flour mixture just until moistened. Spread batter into prepared pan.

5. Bake 20 to 25 minutes or until toothpick inserted in center comes out clean. Cut into 9 squares; serve warm.

Makes 9 servings

Nutrients Per Serving:			
Calories	150	Sodium	370 mg
Total Fat	0.5 g	Cholesterol	0 mg
% of Calories From Fat	3		

Hot Cross Buns

BUNS

1 package active dry yeast
½ cup plus 1 tablespoon
    granulated sugar, divided
¼ cup warm water (105°-115°F)
1 egg
1 cup currants
½ cup Mott's Chunky Apple
    Sauce

¼ cup skim milk
2 tablespoons margarine, melted
1 tablespoon grated lemon peel
1 teaspoon ground cinnamon
½ teaspoon salt
½ teaspoon ground nutmeg
4 cups all-purpose flour
1 egg white, lightly beaten

GLAZE

1 cup powdered sugar
1 tablespoon skim milk

1 tablespoon Mott's Apple Juice

1. **To prepare Buns,** in small bowl, sprinkle yeast and 1 tablespoon granulated sugar over warm water; stir until yeast dissolves. Let stand 5 minutes or until mixture is bubbly.

2. In large bowl, stir together remaining ½ cup granulated sugar and egg. Add currants, apple sauce, ¼ cup milk, margarine, lemon peel, cinnamon, salt and nutmeg; mix well. Stir in yeast mixture. Stir in flour, 1 cup at a time, until soft dough forms.

3. Turn out dough onto floured surface; flatten slightly. Knead 5 minutes or until smooth and elastic, adding any remaining flour to prevent sticking if necessary. Shape dough into ball; place dough in large bowl sprayed with nonstick cooking spray. Turn dough over so that top is greased. Cover with damp towel; let rise in warm place 1½ to 2 hours or until doubled in bulk.

4. Spray 13×9-inch baking pan with nonstick cooking spray. Punch down dough. Cut dough into 12 pieces; shape each piece into a ball. Place balls 1 inch apart in prepared pan. Cover with damp towel; let rise in warm place 30 minutes.

5. Preheat oven to 375°F. Cut cross in top of each bun, ½ inch deep, with tip of sharp knife. Brush top of each bun with egg white.

6. Bake 25 to 30 minutes or until lightly browned and buns sound hollow when tapped. Immediately remove from pan; cool 10 minutes on wire rack.

7. **To prepare Glaze,** in small bowl, combine powdered sugar, 1 tablespoon milk and apple juice until smooth. Drizzle cross design over top of each bun. Serve warm. *Makes 12 servings*

Nutrients Per Serving:

Calories	290	Sodium	130 mg
Total Fat	3.0 g	Cholesterol	20 mg
% of Calories From Fat	9		

Oatmeal Apple Cranberry Scones

2 cups all-purpose flour
1 cup uncooked rolled oats
⅓ cup sugar
2 teaspoons baking powder
½ teaspoon salt
½ teaspoon baking soda
½ teaspoon ground cinnamon
¾ cup Mott's Natural Apple Sauce, divided

2 tablespoons margarine
½ cup coarsely chopped cranberries
½ cup peeled, chopped apple
¼ cup skim milk
¼ cup plus 2 tablespoons honey, divided

1. Preheat oven to 425°F. Spray baking sheet with nonstick cooking spray.

2. In large bowl, combine flour, oats, sugar, baking powder, salt, baking soda and cinnamon. Add ½ cup apple sauce and margarine; cut in with pastry blender or fork until mixture resembles coarse crumbs. Stir in cranberries and apple.

3. In small bowl, combine milk and ¼ cup honey. Add milk mixture to flour mixture; stir together until dough forms a ball.

4. Turn out dough onto well-floured surface; knead 10 to 12 times. Pat dough into 8-inch circle. Place on prepared baking sheet. Use tip of knife to score dough into 12 wedges.

5. In another small bowl, combine remaining ¼ cup apple sauce and 2 tablespoons honey. Brush mixture over top of dough.

6. Bake 12 to 15 minutes or until lightly browned. Immediately remove from baking sheet; cool on wire rack 10 minutes. Serve warm or cool completely. Cut into 12 wedges. *Makes 12 servings*

Nutrients Per Serving:			
Calories	170	Sodium	200 mg
Total Fat	2.5 g	Cholesterol	0 mg
% of Calories From Fat	13		

Oatmeal Apple Cranberry Scones

Apple and Raisin Fruit Braid

SWEET BREAD
- ¼ cup granulated sugar
- 1 package active dry yeast
- ½ cup warm water (105°-115°F)
- 3 cups all-purpose flour, divided
- 2 egg whites
- ¼ cup Mott's Natural Apple Sauce, at room temperature
- 3 tablespoons instant nonfat dry milk
- ¼ teaspoon salt

APPLE AND RAISIN FILLING
- 2½ cups Mott's Chunky Apple Sauce
- ¾ cup raisins
- ¼ cup firmly packed light brown sugar
- ½ teaspoon ground cinnamon
- 2 tablespoons evaporated skim milk

DRIZZLE ICING
- ½ cup powdered sugar
- ¼ cup skim milk

1. **To prepare Sweet Bread,** in large bowl, sprinkle granulated sugar and yeast over warm water; stir until yeast dissolves. Let stand 5 minutes or until mixture is bubbly. Add 1½ cups flour, egg whites, ¼ cup apple sauce, dry milk and salt. Beat with electric mixer at medium speed until combined. Scrape down sides of bowl; continue beating 2 minutes.

2. Stir in enough remaining flour (about 1 cup) until soft dough forms. Turn out dough onto floured surface; flatten slightly. Knead 6 to 8 minutes or until smooth and elastic, adding remaining ½ cup flour to prevent sticking if necessary. Shape dough into ball; place in large bowl sprayed with nonstick cooking spray. Turn dough over so that top is greased. Cover with towel; let rise in warm place 45 to 60 minutes or until doubled in bulk.

3. **To prepare Apple and Raisin Filling,** while dough is rising, in medium saucepan, combine 2½ cups apple sauce, raisins, brown sugar and cinnamon. Cook over medium heat 10 to 15 minutes, stirring frequently. Allow to cool while dough rises.

4. Punch down dough; turn out onto lightly floured surface. Let rest 5 minutes. Spray baking sheet with nonstick cooking spray. Roll out dough into 14×9-inch rectangle; transfer to prepared baking sheet.

5. Spoon filling lengthwise down center of dough in 3-inch-wide strip. Make 2-inch cuts at 1-inch intervals on long sides of rectangle. Fold strips over filling, alternating from left and right and overlapping strips in center to form braided pattern. Tuck ends of last strips under braid.

6. Cover with towel; let rise in warm place about 30 minutes or until doubled in bulk. Preheat oven to 350°F. Uncover; brush top of braid with 2 tablespoons milk.

7. Bake 30 to 35 minutes or until lightly browned and braid sounds hollow when tapped. Immediately remove from baking sheet; cool completely on wire rack.

8. **To prepare Drizzle Icing,** in small bowl, combine powdered sugar and ¼ cup milk until smooth. Drizzle over bread. Cut into 18 slices.

Makes 18 servings

Nutrients Per Serving:

Calories	170	Sodium	45 mg
Total Fat	0.5 g	Cholesterol	0 mg
% of Calories From Fat	1		

Banana Bread

2½ cups all-purpose flour	1 cup sugar
2 teaspoons baking powder	½ cup Mott's Natural Apple Sauce
1 teaspoon baking soda	
½ teaspoon ground allspice	3 egg whites
4 ripe medium bananas, mashed (2 cups)	2 tablespoons vegetable oil
	1 teaspoon vanilla extract

1. Preheat oven to 375°F. Spray 8½×4½-inch loaf pan with nonstick cooking spray.

2. In large bowl, combine flour, baking powder, baking soda and allspice.

3. In medium bowl, whisk together bananas, sugar, apple sauce, egg whites, oil and vanilla.

4. Stir apple sauce mixture into flour mixture just until moistened. Spread batter into prepared pan.

5. Bake 60 minutes or until toothpick inserted in center comes out clean. Cool in pan 10 minutes. Invert onto wire rack; turn right side up. Cool completely. Cut into 16 slices.

Makes 16 servings

Nutrients Per Serving:

Calories	170	Sodium	100 mg
Total Fat	2.0 g	Cholesterol	0 mg
% of Calories From Fat	11		

Apricot Carrot Bread

1¾ cups all-purpose flour
1 teaspoon baking powder
¼ teaspoon baking soda
¼ teaspoon salt
½ cup granulated sugar
½ cup finely shredded carrots
½ cup Mott's Natural Apple Sauce

1 egg, beaten lightly
2 tablespoons vegetable oil
⅓ cup dried apricots, snipped into small bits
½ cup powdered sugar
2 teaspoons Mott's Apple Juice

1. Preheat oven to 350°F. Spray 8×4-inch loaf pan with nonstick cooking spray.

2. In large bowl, combine flour, baking powder, baking soda and salt.

3. In small bowl, combine granulated sugar, carrots, apple sauce, egg and oil.

4. Stir apple sauce mixture into flour mixture just until moistened. (Batter will be thick.) Fold in apricots. Spread batter into prepared pan.

5. Bake 45 to 50 minutes or until toothpick inserted in center comes out clean. Cool in pan 10 minutes. Invert onto wire rack; turn right side up. Cool completely. For best flavor, wrap loaf in plastic wrap or foil; store at room temperature overnight.

6. Just before serving, in small bowl, combine powdered sugar and apple juice until smooth. Drizzle over top of loaf. Cut into 12 slices.

Makes 12 servings

Nutrients Per Serving:			
Calories	160	Sodium	95 mg
Total Fat	3.0 g	Cholesterol	20 mg
% of Calories From Fat	16		

Apricot Carrot Bread

Apple Sauce Coffee Ring

BREAD
1 package active dry yeast
⅓ cup plus 1 teaspoon granulated
    sugar, divided
¼ cup warm water (105°-115°F)
½ cup skim milk
½ cup Mott's Natural Apple
    Sauce

1 egg
2 tablespoons margarine, melted
    and cooled
1 teaspoon salt
1 teaspoon grated lemon peel
5 cups all-purpose flour
1 teaspoon skim milk

FILLING
1½ cups Mott's Chunky Apple
    Sauce
½ cup raisins

⅓ cup firmly packed light brown
    sugar
1 teaspoon ground cinnamon

GLAZE
1 cup powdered sugar
2 tablespoons skim milk

1 teaspoon vanilla extract

1. **To prepare Bread,** in large bowl, sprinkle yeast and 1 teaspoon granulated sugar over warm water; stir until yeast dissolves. Let stand 5 minutes or until mixture is bubbly. Stir in ½ cup milk, ½ cup apple sauce, remaining ⅓ cup granulated sugar, egg, margarine, salt and lemon peel.

2. Stir in flour, 1 cup at a time, until soft dough forms. Turn out dough onto floured surface; flatten slightly. Knead 5 minutes or until smooth and elastic, adding any remaining flour to prevent sticking if necessary. Shape dough into ball; place in large bowl sprayed with nonstick cooking spray. Turn dough over so that top is greased. Cover with damp towel; let rise in warm place 1 hour or until doubled in bulk.

3. Punch down dough. Roll out dough on floured surface into 15-inch square. Spray baking sheet with nonstick cooking spray.

4. **To prepare Filling,** in small bowl, combine 1½ cups apple sauce, raisins, brown sugar and cinnamon. Spread filling over dough, to within ½ inch of edges. Roll up dough jelly-roll style. Moisten edge with water; pinch to seal seam. Moisten ends of dough with water; bring together to form ring. Pinch to seal seam. Place on prepared baking sheet. Make ⅛-inch-deep cuts across width of dough at 2-inch intervals around ring.

5. Let dough rise in warm place, uncovered, 30 minutes.

continued on page 24

Apple Sauce Coffee Ring

Apple Sauce Coffee Ring, continued

6. Preheat oven to 350°F. Brush top lightly with 1 teaspoon milk.

7. Bake 45 to 50 minutes or until lightly browned and ring sounds hollow when tapped. Remove from baking sheet; cool completely on wire rack.

8. **To prepare Glaze,** in small bowl, combine powdered sugar, 2 tablespoons milk and vanilla until smooth. Drizzle over top of ring. Cut into 24 slices. *Makes 24 servings*

Nutrients Per Serving:			
Calories	170	Sodium	110 mg
Total Fat	1.5 g	Cholesterol	10 mg
% of Calories From Fat	8		

Zucchini and Date Tea Loaf

1½ cups all-purpose flour
1 cup sugar
1 teaspoon ground cinnamon
½ teaspoon baking soda
½ teaspoon baking powder
½ teaspoon ground nutmeg

1 cup shredded zucchini
¼ cup Mott's Natural Apple Sauce
2 egg whites, lightly beaten
½ teaspoon grated lemon peel
¼ cup chopped dates

1. Preheat oven to 350°F. Spray 8×4-inch loaf pan with nonstick cooking spray.

2. In large bowl, combine flour, sugar, cinnamon, baking soda, baking powder and nutmeg.

3. In small bowl, combine zucchini, apple sauce, egg whites and lemon peel.

4. Stir apple sauce mixture into flour mixture just until moistened. Fold in dates. Spread batter into prepared pan.

5. Bake 40 to 50 minutes or until toothpick inserted in center comes out clean. Cool in pan 10 minutes. Invert onto wire rack; turn right side up. Cool completely. Cut into 12 slices. *Makes 12 servings*

Nutrients Per Serving:			
Calories	140	Sodium	55 mg
Total Fat	0.5 g	Cholesterol	0 mg
% of Calories From Fat	1		

Morning Glory Bread

2½ cups all-purpose flour
2 teaspoons baking powder
1 teaspoon baking soda
½ teaspoon salt
½ teaspoon ground cinnamon
¼ teaspoon ground nutmeg
¼ teaspoon ground allspice
¾ cup granulated sugar
¾ cup firmly packed light brown sugar
½ cup Mott's Chunky Apple Sauce

3 egg whites
1 tablespoon vegetable oil
1 tablespoon Grandma's Molasses
¾ cup finely shredded carrots
½ cup raisins
⅓ cup drained, crushed pineapple in juice
¼ cup shredded coconut

1. Preheat oven to 375°F. Spray 8½×4½-inch loaf pan with nonstick cooking spray.

2. In large bowl, combine flour, baking powder, baking soda, salt, cinnamon, nutmeg and allspice.

3. In medium bowl, combine granulated sugar, brown sugar, apple sauce, egg whites, oil and molasses.

4. Stir apple sauce mixture into flour mixture just until moistened. Fold in carrots, raisins, pineapple and coconut. Spread into prepared pan.

5. Bake 45 to 50 minutes or until toothpick inserted in center comes out clean. Cool in pan 10 minutes. Invert onto wire rack; turn right side up. Cool completely. Cut into 16 slices. *Makes 16 servings*

Nutrients Per Serving:			
Calories	190	Sodium	170 mg
Total Fat	2.0 g	Cholesterol	0 mg
% of Calories From Fat	7		

Lemon Poppy Seed Tea Loaf

TEA LOAF
2½ cups all-purpose flour
¼ cup poppy seeds
1 tablespoon grated lemon peel
2 teaspoons baking powder
½ teaspoon baking soda
½ teaspoon salt
1 cup sugar

⅔ cup Mott's Natural Apple Sauce
1 whole egg
2 egg whites, lightly beaten
2 tablespoons vegetable oil
1 teaspoon vanilla extract
⅓ cup skim milk

LEMON SYRUP
¼ cup lemon juice

¼ cup sugar

1. Preheat oven to 350°F. Spray 9×5-inch loaf pan with nonstick cooking spray.

2. **To prepare Tea Loaf,** in large bowl, combine flour, poppy seeds, lemon peel, baking powder, baking soda and salt.

3. In medium bowl, combine 1 cup sugar, apple sauce, whole egg, egg whites, oil and vanilla.

4. Stir apple sauce mixture into flour mixture alternately with milk. Mix until thoroughly moistened. Spread batter into prepared pan.

5. Bake 40 to 45 minutes or until toothpick inserted in center comes out clean. Cool in pan 10 minutes. Invert onto wire rack; turn right side up.

6. **To prepare Lemon Syrup,** in small saucepan, combine lemon juice and ¼ cup sugar. Cook, stirring frequently, until sugar dissolves. Cool slightly.

7. Pierce top of loaf with metal skewer. Brush lemon syrup over loaf. Let stand until cool. Cut into 16 slices.

Makes 16 servings

Nutrients Per Serving:			
Calories	170	Sodium	140 mg
Total Fat	3.0 g	Cholesterol	15 mg
% of Calories From Fat	17		

Left to right: Lemon Poppy Seed Tea Loaf, Morning Glory Bread (page 25)

Apple Sauce Irish Soda Bread

3 cups all-purpose flour
1 tablespoon sugar
2 teaspoons baking soda
1 teaspoon salt
1 cup low fat buttermilk

½ cup Mott's Natural Apple
   Sauce
2 tablespoons margarine, melted
½ cup raisins
2 tablespoons skim milk

1. Preheat oven to 375°F. Spray 8-inch round baking pan with nonstick cooking spray.

2. In large bowl, combine flour, sugar, baking soda and salt.

3. In small bowl, combine buttermilk, apple sauce and margarine.

4. Add apple sauce mixture to flour mixture; stir until mixture forms a ball.

5. Turn out dough onto well-floured surface; knead raisins into dough. Pat into 7-inch round.

6. Place dough in prepared pan. Cut cross in top of dough, ¼ inch deep, with tip of sharp knife. Brush top of dough with milk.

7. Bake 35 minutes or until toothpick inserted in center comes out clean. Cool in pan 10 minutes. Invert onto wire rack; turn right side up. Cool completely. Cut into 16 wedges.   *Makes 16 servings*

Nutrients Per Serving:			
Calories	130	Sodium	270 mg
Total Fat	2.0 g	Cholesterol	0 mg
% of Calories From Fat	13		

Apple Sauce Irish Soda Bread

Cinnamania Bread

BREAD

1 cup chopped dates
½ cup water
½ cup Grandma's Molasses
1 (4-ounce) container red hot cinnamon imperial candies
½ cup Mott's Natural Apple Sauce

2 egg whites
1½ cups whole wheat flour
½ cup unprocessed bran
1 tablespoon ground cinnamon
1 teaspoon baking soda
1 teaspoon baking powder

TOPPING

¼ cup Mott's Natural Apple Sauce

½ teaspoon ground cinnamon
¼ cup chopped walnuts

1. Preheat oven to 350°F. Spray 8½×4½-inch loaf pan with nonstick cooking spray.

2. **To prepare Bread,** in medium saucepan, combine dates, water, molasses and candies. Cook over medium heat until mixture boils, stirring constantly. Stir in ½ cup apple sauce; let cool 15 minutes. Stir in egg whites.

3. In large bowl, combine flour, bran, 1 tablespoon cinnamon, baking soda and baking powder.

4. Stir apple sauce mixture into flour mixture just until moistened. Spread batter into prepared pan.

5. **To prepare Topping,** in small bowl, combine ¼ cup apple sauce and ½ teaspoon cinnamon. Spread evenly over top of batter. Sprinkle walnuts over top.

6. Bake 1 hour or until toothpick inserted in center comes out clean. Cool in pan 10 minutes. Invert onto wire rack; turn right side up. Cool completely. Cut into 9 slices.   *Makes 9 servings*

Nutrients Per Serving:			
Calories	250	Sodium	170 mg
Total Fat	3.0 g	Cholesterol	0 mg
% of Calories From Fat	9		

Apple Cinnamon Bowknots

BOWKNOTS
- ¾ cup low fat buttermilk
- 1 egg
- 2 cups all-purpose flour
- ¼ cup uncooked rolled oats
- ⅓ cup plus 2 tablespoons granulated sugar, divided
- 1 teaspoon baking powder
- 1 teaspoon ground cinnamon
- ½ teaspoon baking soda
- ½ teaspoon salt
- ½ cup Mott's Natural Apple Sauce, divided
- 2 tablespoons margarine
- ½ cup peeled, chopped apple
- ⅓ cup raisins
- ¼ cup skim milk

GLAZE
- 1 cup powdered sugar
- 2 tablespoons skim milk
- ½ teaspoon vanilla extract

1. Preheat oven to 350°F. Spray baking sheet with nonstick cooking spray.

2. **To prepare Bowknots,** in small bowl, combine buttermilk and egg.

3. In large bowl, combine flour, oats, ⅓ cup granulated sugar, baking powder, cinnamon, baking soda and salt. Add ¼ cup apple sauce and margarine; cut in with pastry blender or fork until mixture resembles coarse crumbs. Stir in apple and raisins.

4. Make well in center of dry ingredients; add buttermilk mixture. Stir together until dough forms a ball.

5. Turn out dough onto well-floured surface; knead 10 to 12 times. Divide dough into halves; cut each half into 4 equal pieces. Roll each piece into 12-inch-long rope. Cut each rope into two 6-inch-long pieces. Curve each rope into a circle; cross ends at top to form a knot.

6. Combine ¼ cup milk and remaining ¼ cup apple sauce in small bowl. Brush top of each bowknot with mixture. Sprinkle lightly with remaining 2 tablespoons granulated sugar. Place on prepared baking sheet.

7. Place in oven; *increase oven temperature to 425°F.* Bake 12 minutes or until lightly browned. Immediately remove from baking sheet; cool completely on wire rack.

8. **To prepare Glaze,** in small bowl, combine powdered sugar, 2 tablespoons milk and vanilla until smooth. Drizzle over cooled bowknots.

Makes 16 servings

Nutrients Per Serving:			
Calories	150	Sodium	150 mg
Total Fat	2.0 g	Cholesterol	15 mg
% of Calories From Fat	13		

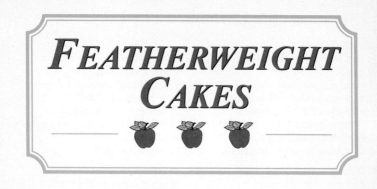

FEATHERWEIGHT CAKES

Guilt-Free Black Forest Cake

3 cups all-purpose flour
2½ cups sugar
⅓ cup unsweetened cocoa
    powder
2 teaspoons baking soda
1 teaspoon salt
2 cups cold water
¾ cup Mott's Natural Apple
    Sauce
2 eggs
2 tablespoons apple-cider
    vinegar

1 tablespoon vanilla extract
1 (1.4-ounce) package sugar-free
    instant chocolate pudding
2 cups skim milk
1 (20-ounce) can light cherry pie
    filling
  Frozen light nondairy
    whipped topping, thawed
    (optional)

1. Preheat oven to 350°F. Spray 13×9-inch pan with nonstick cooking spray.

2. In medium bowl, combine flour, sugar, cocoa, baking soda and salt.

3. In large bowl, combine water, apple sauce, eggs, vinegar and vanilla.

4. Add flour mixture to apple sauce mixture; stir until well blended. Pour batter into prepared pan.

5. Bake 45 minutes or until toothpick inserted in center comes out clean. Cool completely on wire rack.

continued on page 34

Guilt-Free Black Forest Cake

Guilt-Free Black Forest Cake, continued

6. Prepare pudding mix according to package directions using 2 cups skim milk.

7. Spread top of cake with pudding; refrigerate until set. Top evenly with dollops of pie filling; spread over pudding. Cut into 10 pieces. Serve with whipped topping, if desired. Refrigerate leftovers. *Makes 10 servings*

Nutrients Per Serving:			
Calories	450	Sodium	470 mg
Total Fat	2.0 g	Cholesterol	45 mg
% of Calories From Fat	4		

Magic Apple Roll

2 cups Mott's Natural Apple Sauce
½ teaspoon ground cinnamon
4 egg whites
¾ cup granulated sugar
⅔ cup all-purpose flour
¾ teaspoon baking powder
¼ teaspoon salt
1 teaspoon vanilla extract
1 tablespoon powdered sugar

1. Preheat oven to 400°F. Spray 15×10-inch jelly-roll pan with nonstick cooking spray. Line with waxed paper; spray paper with cooking spray. Pour apple sauce into pan, spreading evenly. Sprinkle with cinnamon.

2. In large bowl, beat egg whites with electric mixer at high speed until foamy. Gradually add granulated sugar, beating until mixture is thick and light.

3. In small bowl, sift together flour, baking powder and salt. Fold into egg white mixture with vanilla. Gently pour batter over apple sauce mixture, spreading evenly.

4. Bake 15 to 18 minutes or until lightly browned. Cool on wire rack 5 minutes. Invert cake, apple sauce side up, onto clean, lint-free dish towel sprinkled with powdered sugar; peel off waxed paper. Trim edges of cake. Starting at narrow end, roll up cake. Place, seam side down, on serving plate. Cool completely. Sprinkle top with powdered sugar. Cut into 10 slices. *Makes 10 servings*

Nutrients Per Serving:			
Calories	120	Sodium	100 mg
Total Fat	0.5 g	Cholesterol	0 mg
% of Calories From Fat	1		

Orange Tunnel Cake

CAKE
2¼ cups all-purpose flour
1 tablespoon baking powder
1 teaspoon salt
½ teaspoon baking soda
1 cup granulated sugar
2 tablespoons margarine, softened
5 egg whites

½ cup Mott's Natural Apple Sauce
1 tablespoon grated orange peel
2 tablespoons orange juice
1 teaspoon orange extract
1 (0.9-ounce) package sugar-free instant vanilla pudding
1½ cups skim milk

GLAZE
2 cups powdered sugar, sifted
1 tablespoon grated orange peel

2 tablespoons orange juice

1. Preheat oven to 375°F. Spray 10-inch (12-cup) Bundt pan with nonstick cooking spray.

2. **To prepare Cake,** in medium bowl, sift together flour, baking powder, salt and baking soda.

3. In large bowl, beat granulated sugar and margarine with electric mixer at medium speed until blended. Whisk in egg whites, apple sauce, 1 tablespoon orange peel, 2 tablespoons orange juice and orange extract.

4. Add flour mixture to apple sauce mixture; stir until well blended.

5. Prepare pudding mix according to package directions using 1½ cups skim milk.

6. Pour half of batter into prepared pan. Spoon vanilla pudding in ring in center of cake, to within ½ inch of inside and outside edges of pan. Gently spoon remaining batter over pudding.

7. Bake 50 to 55 minutes or until lightly browned. Cool on wire rack 15 minutes before removing from pan. Place cake, fluted side up, on serving plate. Cool completely.

8. **To prepare Glaze,** in medium bowl, combine powdered sugar, 1 tablespoon orange peel and 2 tablespoons orange juice until smooth. Add water, 1 teaspoon at a time, until of desired consistency. Drizzle over cooled cake. Cut into 14 slices. Refrigerate leftovers.   *Makes 14 servings*

Lemon Tunnel Cake: Substitute grated lemon peel, lemon juice and lemon extract for the grated orange peel, orange juice and orange extract.

Nutrients Per Serving:			
Calories	230	Sodium	310 mg
Total Fat	2.0 g	Cholesterol	0 mg
% of Calories From Fat	8		

Pineapple Upside-Down Cake

1 (8-ounce) can crushed
   pineapple in juice,
   undrained
2 tablespoons margarine,
   melted, divided
½ cup firmly packed light brown
   sugar
6 whole maraschino cherries

1½ cups all-purpose flour
2 tablespoons baking powder
¼ teaspoon salt
1 cup granulated sugar
½ cup Mott's Natural Apple
   Sauce
1 whole egg
3 egg whites, beaten until stiff

1. Preheat oven to 375°F. Drain pineapple; reserve juice. Spray sides of 8-inch square baking pan with nonstick cooking spray.

2. Spread 1 tablespoon melted margarine evenly in bottom of prepared pan. Sprinkle with brown sugar; top with pineapple. Slice cherries in half. Arrange cherries, cut side up, so that when cake is cut, each piece will have cherry half in center.

3. In small bowl, combine flour, baking powder and salt.

4. In large bowl, combine granulated sugar, apple sauce, whole egg, remaining 1 tablespoon melted margarine and reserved pineapple juice.

5. Add flour mixture to apple sauce mixture; stir until well blended. Fold in egg whites. Gently pour batter over fruit, spreading evenly.

6. Bake 35 to 40 minutes or until lightly browned. Cool on wire rack 10 minutes. Invert cake onto serving plate. Serve warm or cool completely. Cut into 12 pieces. *Makes 12 servings*

Nutrients Per Serving:			
Calories	200	Sodium	240 mg
Total Fat	2.5 g	Cholesterol	20 mg
% of Calories From Fat	11		

Pineapple Upside-Down Cake

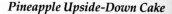

Peppermint Cake

CAKE

2¼ cups cake flour
 2 teaspoons baking powder
 1 teaspoon salt
 ½ teaspoon baking soda
1½ cups sugar
 2 tablespoons margarine,
   softened

½ cup Mott's Natural Apple
   Sauce
½ cup skim milk
 4 egg whites
 1 teaspoon vanilla extract

PEPPERMINT FROSTING

1½ cups sugar
 ¼ cup water
 2 egg whites
 ¼ teaspoon cream of tartar

½ teaspoon peppermint extract
 3 tablespoons crushed starlight
   candies (about 6)

1. Preheat oven to 350°F. Spray 9-inch round cake pan with nonstick cooking spray.

2. **To prepare Cake,** in medium bowl, combine flour, baking powder, salt and baking soda. In large bowl, beat 1½ cups sugar and margarine with electric mixer at medium speed until blended. Whisk in apple sauce, milk, 4 egg whites and vanilla.

3. Add flour mixture to apple sauce mixture; stir until well blended. Pour batter into prepared pan.

4. Bake 35 to 40 minutes or until toothpick inserted in center comes out clean. Cool completely on wire rack. Split cake horizontally in half to make 2 layers.

5. **To prepare Peppermint Frosting,** in top of double boiler, whisk together 1½ cups sugar, water, 2 egg whites and cream of tartar. Cook, whisking occasionally, over simmering water 4 minutes or until mixture is hot and sugar is dissolved. Remove from heat; stir in peppermint extract. Beat with electric mixer at high speed 3 minutes or until mixture forms stiff peaks.

6. Place one cake layer on serving plate. Spread with layer of Peppermint Frosting. Top with second cake layer. Frost top and side with remaining Peppermint Frosting. Sprinkle top and side of cake with crushed candies. Cut into 12 slices. Refrigerate leftovers. *Makes 12 servings*

Nutrients Per Serving:			
Calories	300	Sodium	320 mg
Total Fat	2.0 g	Cholesterol	0 mg
% of Calories From Fat	6		

Peppermint Cake

Apple-Streusel Pound Cake

3 cups all-purpose flour
⅓ cup cornmeal
1½ teaspoons baking soda
1½ teaspoons baking powder
½ teaspoon salt
1 cup granulated sugar
1 cup skim milk
1 cup nonfat sour cream
½ cup Mott's Natural Apple
    Sauce
1 whole egg
2 tablespoons vegetable oil
2 teaspoons vanilla extract
3 egg whites, beaten until stiff
¾ cup firmly packed light brown
    sugar
¾ cup peeled, chopped apple
½ cup uncooked rolled oats
2 teaspoons ground cinnamon

1. Preheat oven to 350°F. Spray 10-inch (12-cup) Bundt pan with nonstick cooking spray; flour lightly.

2. In medium bowl, combine flour, cornmeal, baking soda, baking powder and salt.

3. In large bowl, combine granulated sugar, milk, sour cream, apple sauce, whole egg, oil and vanilla.

4. Add flour mixture to apple sauce mixture; stir until well blended. Gently fold in beaten egg whites.

5. In small bowl, combine brown sugar, apple, oats and cinnamon.

6. Spread half of batter into prepared pan; sprinkle with oat mixture. Spread remaining batter over oat mixture.

7. Bake 60 to 70 minutes or until toothpick inserted in center comes out clean. Cool on wire rack 15 minutes before removing from pan. Place cake, fluted side up, on serving plate. Serve warm or cool completely. Cut into 24 slices.

Makes 24 servings

Nutrients Per Serving:

Calories	160	Sodium	140 mg
Total Fat	1.5 g	Cholesterol	10 mg
% of Calories From Fat	9		

Raisin-Streusel Coffee Cake

1½ cups all-purpose flour
2 teaspoons baking powder
¼ teaspoon baking soda
¼ teaspoon salt
¾ cup granulated sugar
2 tablespoons margarine, softened
¾ cup nonfat sour cream
1 egg

1 teaspoon vanilla extract
½ cup Mott's Chunky Apple Sauce
⅓ cup firmly packed light brown sugar
¼ cup raisins
2 tablespoons crunchy nut-like cereal nuggets

1. Preheat oven to 350°F. Spray 9-inch round cake pan with nonstick cooking spray.

2. In small bowl, combine flour, baking powder, baking soda and salt.

3. In large bowl, beat granulated sugar and margarine with electric mixer at medium speed until blended. Whisk in sour cream, egg and vanilla. Gently mix in apple sauce.

4. Add flour mixture to apple sauce mixture; stir until well blended. Pour batter into prepared pan.

5. In small bowl, combine brown sugar, raisins and cereal. Sprinkle over batter.

6. Bake 50 minutes or until toothpick inserted in center comes out clean. Cool 15 minutes on wire rack. Serve warm or cool completely. Cut into 14 slices. *Makes 14 servings*

Nutrients Per Serving:			
Calories	160	Sodium	150 mg
Total Fat	2.0 g	Cholesterol	15 mg
% of Calories From Fat	12		

Boston Cream Pie

CAKE

2¼ cups cake flour
2 teaspoons baking powder
1 teaspoon salt
½ teaspoon baking soda
1½ cups granulated sugar
2 tablespoons margarine, softened

½ cup Mott's Natural Apple Sauce
½ cup skim milk
4 egg whites
1 teaspoon vanilla extract

FILLING

1 (0.9-ounce) package sugar-free instant vanilla pudding

1½ cups skim milk

CHOCOLATE GLAZE

1½ cups powdered sugar
2 tablespoons unsweetened cocoa powder

1 tablespoon skim milk
½ teaspoon vanilla extract
Lemon peel strips (optional)

1. Preheat oven to 350°F. Spray 9-inch round cake pan with nonstick cooking spray.

2. **To prepare Cake,** in medium bowl, combine flour, baking powder, salt and baking soda.

3. In large bowl, beat granulated sugar and margarine with electric mixer at medium speed until blended. Whisk in apple sauce, ½ cup milk, egg whites and 1 teaspoon vanilla.

4. Add flour mixture to apple sauce mixture; stir until well blended. Pour batter into prepared pan.

5. Bake 35 to 40 minutes or until toothpick inserted in center comes out clean. Cool completely on wire rack. Split cake horizontally in half to make 2 layers.

6. **To prepare Filling,** prepare pudding mix according to package directions using 1½ cups skim milk. (Or, substitute 1½ cups prepared fat-free vanilla pudding for Filling.)

continued on page 44

Boston Cream Pie, continued

7. **To prepare Chocolate Glaze,** in small bowl, sift together powdered sugar and cocoa. Stir in 1 tablespoon milk and ½ teaspoon vanilla. Add water, 1 teaspoon at a time, until of desired spreading consistency. Place one cake layer on serving plate. Spread filling over cake. Top with second cake layer. Spread top of cake with Chocolate Glaze. Let stand until set. Garnish with lemon peel, if desired. Cut into 10 slices. Refrigerate leftovers.

Makes 10 servings

Nutrients Per Serving:			
Calories	330	Sodium	410 mg
Total Fat	3.0 g	Cholesterol	0 mg
% of Calories From Fat	8		

Cocoa Molasses Bundt Cake

1¾ cups all-purpose flour
3 tablespoons unsweetened cocoa powder
1½ teaspoons baking powder
1½ teaspoons baking soda
½ teaspoon salt
1½ cups low fat buttermilk

1 cup granulated sugar
½ cup Mott's Apple Sauce
½ cup Grandma's Molasses
1 whole egg
2 tablespoons margarine, melted
3 egg whites, beaten until stiff
Powdered sugar (optional)

1. Preheat oven to 350°F. Spray 10-inch (12-cup) Bundt pan with nonstick cooking spray; flour lightly.

2. In small bowl, combine flour, cocoa, baking powder, baking soda and salt.

3. In large bowl, combine buttermilk, granulated sugar, apple sauce, molasses, whole egg and margarine.

4. Beat flour mixture into apple sauce mixture with electric mixer at low speed until moistened. Beat on high speed 3 minutes. Gently fold in beaten egg whites. Pour batter into prepared pan.

5. Bake 55 minutes or until toothpick inserted in center comes out clean. Cool on wire rack 15 minutes before removing from pan. Place cake, fluted side up, on serving plate. Cool completely. Sprinkle powdered sugar over top of cake, if desired. Cut into 12 slices.

Makes 12 servings

Nutrients Per Serving:			
Calories	210	Sodium	310 mg
Total Fat	3.0 g	Cholesterol	20 mg
% of Calories From Fat	13		

Moist and Spicy Prune Cake

CAKE
- 1 cup pitted, stewed prunes
- 2 cups all-purpose flour
- 1 teaspoon baking soda
- 1 teaspoon ground cinnamon
- ½ teaspoon ground cloves
- ½ teaspoon ground nutmeg
- ½ teaspoon ground allspice
- ¼ teaspoon salt
- 1½ cups granulated sugar
- 1 cup Mott's Natural Apple Sauce
- 4 egg whites
- 2 tablespoons vegetable oil
- ½ cup low fat buttermilk

LEMON ALMOND ICING
- 2 cups powdered sugar
- 1½ teaspoons lemon juice
- ¼ teaspoon almond extract

1. Preheat oven to 350°F. Spray 10-inch (12-cup) Bundt pan with nonstick cooking spray.

2. **To prepare Cake,** place prunes in food processor or blender; process until smooth.

3. In medium bowl, sift together flour, baking soda, cinnamon, cloves, nutmeg, allspice and salt.

4. In large bowl, whisk together granulated sugar, apple sauce, egg whites and oil.

5. Add flour mixture to apple sauce mixture alternately with buttermilk; stir until well blended. Add prunes; stir well. Pour batter into prepared pan.

6. Bake 60 minutes or until toothpick inserted in center comes out clean. Cool on wire rack 15 minutes before removing from pan. Place cake, fluted side up, on serving plate. Cool completely.

7. **To prepare Lemon Almond Icing,** in medium bowl, combine powdered sugar, lemon juice and almond extract until smooth. Add water, 1 teaspoon at a time, until of desired consistency. Drizzle over cooled cake. Cut into 14 slices. *Makes 14 servings*

Nutrients Per Serving:			
Calories	260	Sodium	125 mg
Total Fat	2.5 g	Cholesterol	0 mg
% of Calories From Fat	8		

Rocky Road Cake

1¾ cups all-purpose flour
⅓ cup unsweetened cocoa
    powder
2 teaspoons baking powder
1 teaspoon baking soda
½ teaspoon salt
1 cup granulated sugar
¾ cup Mott's Natural Apple
    Sauce
½ cup skim milk

4 egg whites
1 teaspoon vanilla extract
¾ cup marshmallow topping
½ cup frozen light nondairy
    whipped topping, thawed
2 tablespoons chopped unsalted
    peanuts
Powdered sugar (optional)
Fresh red currants (optional)
Mint leaves (optional)

1. Preheat oven to 350°F. Line 15½×10½-inch jelly-roll pan with waxed paper.

2. In medium bowl, sift together flour, cocoa, baking powder, baking soda and salt.

3. In large bowl, whisk together granulated sugar, apple sauce, milk, egg whites and vanilla.

4. Add flour mixture to apple sauce mixture; stir until well blended. Pour batter into prepared pan.

5. Bake 12 to 15 minutes or until top springs back when lightly touched. Immediately invert onto clean, lint-free dish towel sprinkled with powdered sugar; peel off waxed paper. Trim edges of cake. Starting at narrow end, roll up cake and towel together. Cool completely on wire rack.

6. In small bowl, whisk marshmallow topping until softened. Gently fold in whipped topping.

7. Unroll cake; spread with marshmallow mixture to within ½ inch of edges of cake. Sprinkle peanuts over marshmallow mixture. Reroll cake; place, seam side down, on serving plate. Cover; refrigerate 1 hour before slicing. Sprinkle with powdered sugar and garnish with currants and mint leaves, if desired, just before serving. Cut into 14 slices. Refrigerate leftovers.

Makes 14 servings

Nutrients Per Serving:

Calories	190	Sodium	210 mg
Total Fat	1.5 g	Cholesterol	0 mg
% of Calories From Fat	6		

Three-Berry Kuchen

1¾ cups all-purpose flour,
   divided
2 teaspoons baking powder
½ teaspoon baking soda
½ teaspoon salt
⅔ cup Mott's Apple Sauce
4 egg whites
¼ cup nonfat plain yogurt

2 tablespoons granulated sugar
1 teaspoon grated lemon peel
2 cups assorted fresh or thawed,
   frozen blueberries,
   raspberries or blackberries
¼ cup firmly packed light brown
   sugar
2 tablespoons margarine

1. Preheat oven to 350°F. Spray 10-inch round cake pan with nonstick cooking spray.

2. In small bowl, combine 1½ cups flour, baking powder, baking soda and salt.

3. In large bowl, whisk together apple sauce, egg whites, yogurt, granulated sugar and lemon peel.

4. Add flour mixture to apple sauce mixture; stir until well blended. Spread batter into prepared pan.

5. Sprinkle berries over batter. Combine remaining ¼ cup flour and brown sugar in small bowl. Cut in margarine with pastry blender or fork until mixture resembles coarse crumbs. Sprinkle over berries.

6. Bake 50 to 55 minutes or until lightly browned. Cool on wire rack 20 minutes. Serve warm or cool completely. Cut into 9 slices.

Makes 9 servings

Nutrients Per Serving:			
Calories	190	Sodium	290 mg
Total Fat	3.0 g	Cholesterol	0 mg
% of Calories From Fat	14		

Three-Berry Kuchen

Holiday Fruit Cake

2 cups dark raisins
1 cup golden raisins
1 cup whole candied red
　　cherries
¼ cup candied pineapple chunks
¼ cup mixed candied fruit
2¼ cups all-purpose flour,
　　divided
1 teaspoon baking powder
½ teaspoon ground nutmeg
½ teaspoon ground cardamom

½ teaspoon ground coriander
1¼ cups firmly packed light
　　brown sugar
1 cup Mott's Natural Apple
　　Sauce
8 egg whites
3 tablespoons honey
1 tablespoon grated orange peel
1 tablespoon grated lemon peel
1 teaspoon vanilla extract
½ cup Mott's Apple Juice

1. Preheat oven to 300°F. Spray 9-inch springform pan with nonstick cooking spray. Line pan with waxed paper, extending paper at least 1 inch above rim of pan. Spray waxed paper with nonstick cooking spray.

2. In medium bowl, combine dark raisins, golden raisins, cherries, pineapple and mixed fruit. Toss with ¼ cup flour.

3. In another medium bowl, combine remaining 2 cups flour, baking powder, nutmeg, cardamom and coriander.

4. In large bowl, combine brown sugar, apple sauce, egg whites, honey, orange peel, lemon peel and vanilla.

5. Add flour mixture to apple sauce mixture alternately with apple juice; stir just until blended. Fold in fruit mixture. Pour batter into prepared pan.

6. Bake 2 hours or until toothpick inserted in center comes out clean and cake is firm to the touch. Cool completely on wire rack. Remove cake from pan; peel off waxed paper. Wrap cake tightly in aluminum foil; store in refrigerator up to 2 weeks or in freezer up to 2 months. Cut into 20 slices.

Makes 20 servings

Nutrients Per Serving:

Calories	260	Sodium	45 mg
Total Fat	0.5 g	Cholesterol	0 mg
% of Calories From Fat	1		

Carrot Cake

CAKE
- 3 cups all-purpose flour
- 2 teaspoons baking powder
- 1 teaspoon baking soda
- 1 teaspoon ground cinnamon
- ½ teaspoon salt
- 1 cup Mott's Natural Apple Sauce
- 1 cup granulated sugar
- 1 cup firmly packed light brown sugar
- 5 egg whites
- 2 tablespoons vegetable oil
- 1 teaspoon grated orange peel
- 2 tablespoons orange juice
- 3 cups finely shredded carrots
- 1 cup raisins

ORANGE GLAZE
- 2 cups powdered sugar
- 2 tablespoons Mott's Natural Apple Sauce
- 1 teaspoon grated orange peel
- 2 tablespoons orange juice

1. Preheat oven to 350°F. Spray 10-inch (12-cup) Bundt pan with nonstick cooking spray.

2. **To prepare Cake,** in medium bowl, combine flour, baking powder, baking soda, cinnamon and salt.

3. In large bowl, whisk together 1 cup apple sauce, granulated sugar, brown sugar, egg whites, oil, 1 teaspoon orange peel and 2 tablespoons orange juice.

4. Add flour mixture to apple sauce mixture; stir until well blended. Fold in carrots and raisins. Pour batter into prepared pan.

5. Bake 60 to 65 minutes or until toothpick inserted in center comes out clean. Cool on wire rack 15 minutes before removing from pan. Place cake, fluted side up, on serving plate. Cool completely.

6. **To prepare Orange Glaze,** in medium bowl, combine powdered sugar, 2 tablespoons apple sauce, 1 teaspoon orange peel and 2 tablespoons orange juice until smooth. Drizzle over cooled cake. Cut into 14 slices.

Makes 14 servings

Nutrients Per Serving:			
Calories	350	Sodium	220 mg
Total Fat	2.5 g	Cholesterol	0 mg
% of Calories From Fat	6		

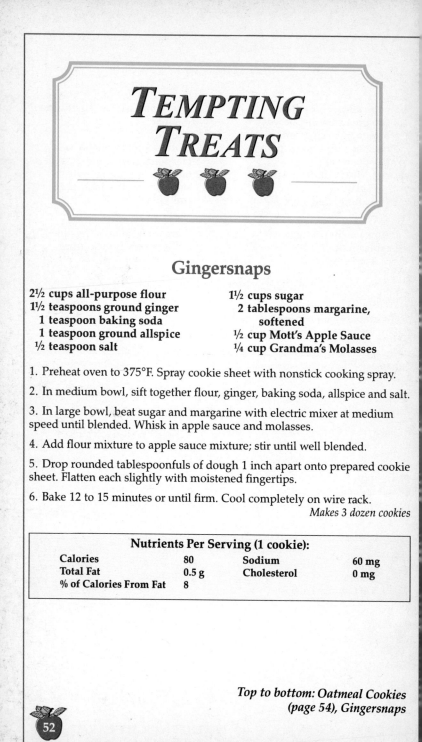

TEMPTING TREATS

Gingersnaps

2½ cups all-purpose flour
1½ teaspoons ground ginger
1 teaspoon baking soda
1 teaspoon ground allspice
½ teaspoon salt

1½ cups sugar
2 tablespoons margarine, softened
½ cup Mott's Apple Sauce
¼ cup Grandma's Molasses

1. Preheat oven to 375°F. Spray cookie sheet with nonstick cooking spray.

2. In medium bowl, sift together flour, ginger, baking soda, allspice and salt.

3. In large bowl, beat sugar and margarine with electric mixer at medium speed until blended. Whisk in apple sauce and molasses.

4. Add flour mixture to apple sauce mixture; stir until well blended.

5. Drop rounded tablespoonfuls of dough 1 inch apart onto prepared cookie sheet. Flatten each slightly with moistened fingertips.

6. Bake 12 to 15 minutes or until firm. Cool completely on wire rack.

Makes 3 dozen cookies

Nutrients Per Serving (1 cookie):

Calories	80	Sodium	60 mg
Total Fat	0.5 g	Cholesterol	0 mg
% of Calories From Fat	8		

Top to bottom: Oatmeal Cookies (page 54), Gingersnaps

Oatmeal Cookies

1 cup all-purpose flour
1 teaspoon baking powder
½ teaspoon baking soda
½ teaspoon salt
¼ cup Mott's Cinnamon Apple
  Sauce
2 tablespoons margarine

½ cup granulated sugar
½ cup firmly packed light brown
  sugar
1 egg
1 teaspoon vanilla extract
1⅓ cups uncooked rolled oats
½ cup raisins (optional)

1. Preheat oven to 375°F. Spray cookie sheet with nonstick cooking spray.

2. In small bowl, combine flour, baking powder, baking soda and salt.

3. In large bowl, place apple sauce. Cut in margarine with pastry blender or fork until margarine breaks into pea-sized pieces. Add granulated sugar, brown sugar, egg and vanilla; stir until well blended.

4. Add flour mixture to apple sauce mixture; stir until well blended. Fold in oats and raisins, if desired.

5. Drop rounded teaspoonfuls of dough 2 inches apart onto prepared cookie sheet.

6. Bake 10 to 12 minutes or until lightly browned. Cool 5 minutes on cookie sheet. Remove to wire rack; cool completely.   *Makes 3 dozen cookies*

Nutrients Per Serving (1 cookie):			
Calories	60	Sodium	60 mg
Total Fat	1.0 g	Cholesterol	5 mg
% of Calories From Fat	15		

Lemon Bars

CRUST
- 1 cup all-purpose flour
- ½ cup powdered sugar
- ¼ cup Mott's Natural Apple Sauce
- 2 tablespoons margarine, melted

LEMON FILLING
- 1 cup granulated sugar
- 2 egg whites
- 1 whole egg
- ⅓ cup Mott's Natural Apple Sauce
- 1 teaspoon grated lemon peel
- ¼ cup lemon juice
- 3 tablespoons all-purpose flour
- ½ teaspoon baking powder
- Additional powdered sugar (optional)

1. Preheat oven to 350°F. Spray 8-inch square baking pan with nonstick cooking spray.

2. **To prepare Crust,** in small bowl, combine 1 cup flour and powdered sugar. Add ¼ cup apple sauce and margarine. Stir with fork until mixture resembles coarse crumbs. Press evenly into bottom of prepared pan. Bake 10 minutes.

3. **To prepare Lemon Filling,** in medium bowl, beat granulated sugar, egg whites and whole egg with electric mixer at medium speed until thick and smooth. Add ⅓ cup apple sauce, lemon peel, lemon juice, 3 tablespoons flour and baking powder. Beat until well blended. Pour lemon filling over baked crust.

4. Bake 20 to 25 minutes or until lightly browned. Cool completely on wire rack. Sprinkle with additional powdered sugar, if desired; cut into 14 bars.

Makes 14 servings

Nutrients Per Serving:			
Calories	140	Sodium	45 mg
Total Fat	2.0 g	Cholesterol	15 mg
% of Calories From Fat	14		

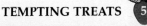

Fabulous Fruit Bars

1½ cups all-purpose flour,
   divided
1½ cups sugar, divided
½ cup Mott's Apple Sauce,
   divided
½ teaspoon baking powder
2 tablespoons margarine
½ cup peeled, chopped apple

½ cup chopped dried apricots
½ cup chopped cranberries
1 whole egg
1 egg white
1 teaspoon lemon juice
½ teaspoon vanilla extract
1 teaspoon ground cinnamon

1. Preheat oven to 350°F. Spray 13×9-inch baking pan with nonstick cooking spray.

2. In medium bowl, combine 1¼ cups flour, ½ cup sugar, ⅓ cup apple sauce and baking powder. Cut in margarine with pastry blender or fork until mixture resembles coarse crumbs.

3. In large bowl, combine apple, apricots, cranberries, remaining apple sauce, whole egg, egg white, lemon juice and vanilla.

4. In small bowl, combine remaining 1 cup sugar, ¼ cup flour and cinnamon. Add to fruit mixture, stirring just until mixed.

5. Press half of crumb mixture evenly into bottom of prepared pan. Top with fruit mixture. Sprinkle with remaining crumb mixture.

6. Bake 40 minutes or until lightly browned. Broil, 4 inches from heat, 1 to 2 minutes or until golden brown. Cool on wire rack 15 minutes; cut into 16 bars.

Makes 16 servings

Nutrients Per Serving:			
Calories	150	Sodium	35 mg
Total Fat	2.0 g	Cholesterol	15 mg
% of Calories From Fat	11		

Fabulous Fruit Bars

Apple Oatmeal Snack Bars

1½ cups all-purpose flour
¾ cup uncooked rolled oats
1 teaspoon baking powder
½ teaspoon salt
1 cup granulated sugar
2 tablespoons margarine,
 softened
½ cup Mott's Cinnamon Apple
 Sauce

1 egg
1 teaspoon vanilla extract
1 cup Mott's Chunky Apple
 Sauce
⅓ cup raisins
1 tablespoon firmly packed light
 brown sugar
½ teaspoon ground cinnamon

1. Preheat oven to 375°F. Spray 8-inch square baking pan with nonstick cooking spray.

2. In medium bowl, combine flour, oats, baking powder and salt.

3. In large bowl, beat granulated sugar and margarine with electric mixer at medium speed until blended. Whisk in ½ cup cinnamon apple sauce, egg and vanilla.

4. Add flour mixture to apple sauce mixture; stir until well blended. Spoon half of batter into prepared pan, spreading evenly.

5. In small bowl, combine 1 cup chunky apple sauce, raisins, brown sugar and cinnamon. Pour evenly over batter.

6. Spoon remaining batter over filling, spreading evenly.

7. Bake 30 to 35 minutes or until lightly browned. Cool on wire rack 15 minutes; cut into 16 bars. *Makes 16 servings*

Nutrients Per Serving:			
Calories	150	Sodium	110 mg
Total Fat	2.0 g	Cholesterol	10 mg
% of Calories From Fat	13		

Apple Oatmeal Snack Bars

Tri-Layer Chocolate Oatmeal Bars

CRUST
1 cup uncooked rolled oats
½ cup all-purpose flour
½ cup firmly packed light brown
  sugar
¼ cup Mott's Natural Apple
  Sauce
1 tablespoon margarine, melted
¼ teaspoon baking soda

FILLING
⅔ cup all-purpose flour
½ teaspoon baking powder
¼ teaspoon salt
¾ cup granulated sugar
¼ cup Mott's Natural Apple
  Sauce
1 whole egg
1 egg white
2 tablespoons unsweetened
  cocoa powder
1 tablespoon margarine, melted
½ teaspoon vanilla extract
¼ cup low fat buttermilk

ICING
1 cup powdered sugar
1 tablespoon unsweetened cocoa
  powder
1 tablespoon skim milk
1 teaspoon instant coffee
  powder

1. Preheat oven to 350°F. Spray 8-inch square baking pan with nonstick cooking spray.

2. **To prepare Crust,** in medium bowl, combine oats, ½ cup flour, brown sugar, ¼ cup apple sauce, 1 tablespoon margarine and baking soda. Stir with fork until mixture resembles coarse crumbs. Press evenly into bottom of prepared pan. Bake 10 minutes.

3. **To prepare Filling,** in small bowl, combine ⅔ cup flour, baking powder and salt.

4. In large bowl, combine granulated sugar, ¼ cup apple sauce, whole egg, egg white, 2 tablespoons cocoa, 1 tablespoon margarine and vanilla.

5. Add flour mixture to apple sauce mixture alternately with buttermilk; stir until well blended. Spread filling over baked crust.

6. Bake 25 minutes or until toothpick inserted in center comes out clean. Cool completely on wire rack.

continued on page 62

Tri-Layer Chocolate Oatmeal Bars, continued

7. **To prepare Icing,** in small bowl, combine powdered sugar, 1 tablespoon cocoa, milk and coffee powder until smooth. Spread evenly over bars. Let stand until set. Run tip of knife through icing to score. Cut into 14 bars.

Makes 14 servings

Nutrients Per Serving:			
Calories	190	Sodium	100 mg
Total Fat	2.5 g	Cholesterol	15 mg
% of Calories From Fat	13		

Jam Thumbprint Gems

1½ cups all-purpose flour
1 teaspoon baking powder
½ teaspoon salt
½ teaspoon ground cinnamon
¼ teaspoon ground cloves
¼ cup Mott's Natural Apple Sauce

2 tablespoons vegetable shortening
½ cup plus 1 tablespoon powdered sugar, divided
1 egg
½ teaspoon vanilla extract
½ cup strawberry or other favorite flavor preserves

1. Preheat oven to 400°F. Spray cookie sheet with nonstick cooking spray.

2. In small bowl, combine flour, baking powder, salt and spices.

3. In large bowl, whisk together apple sauce and shortening until shortening breaks into pea-sized pieces. Add ½ cup powdered sugar; stir well. Add egg and vanilla; mix well.

4. Add flour mixture to apple sauce mixture; stir until well blended. (Mixture will be stiff.)

5. Using flour-coated hands, roll teaspoonfuls of dough into balls. Place 1 inch apart on prepared cookie sheet. Press thumb gently into center of each ball. Spoon ½ teaspoon preserves into each indentation.

6. Bake 12 to 15 minutes or until lightly browned. Cool completely on wire rack; sprinkle with remaining 1 tablespoon powdered sugar.

Makes 2 dozen cookies

Nutrients Per Serving (1 cookie):			
Calories	70	Sodium	60 mg
Total Fat	1.5 g	Cholesterol	10 mg
% of Calories From Fat	17		

Marble Brownies

½ cup plus 2 tablespoons all-purpose flour, divided
½ cup unsweetened cocoa powder
1 teaspoon baking powder
½ teaspoon salt
1¾ cups sugar, divided
2 tablespoons margarine, softened

½ cup Mott's Natural Apple Sauce
3 egg whites, divided
1½ teaspoons vanilla extract, divided
4 ounces low fat cream cheese (Neufchâtel), softened

1. Preheat oven to 350°F. Spray 8-inch square baking pan with nonstick cooking spray.

2. In small bowl, sift together ½ cup flour, cocoa, baking powder and salt.

3. In large bowl, beat 1½ cups sugar and margarine with electric mixer at medium speed until blended. Whisk in apple sauce, 2 egg whites and 1 teaspoon vanilla.

4. Add flour mixture to apple sauce mixture; stir until well blended. Pour batter into prepared pan.

5. In small bowl, beat cream cheese and remaining ¼ cup sugar with electric mixer at medium speed until blended. Stir in remaining egg white, 2 tablespoons flour and ½ teaspoon vanilla. Pour over brownie batter; run knife through batters to marble.

6. Bake 35 to 40 minutes or until firm. Cool on wire rack 15 minutes; cut into 12 bars. *Makes 12 servings*

Nutrients Per Serving:			
Calories	180	Sodium	150 mg
Total Fat	2.5 g	Cholesterol	0 mg
% of Calories From Fat	13		

Pumpkin Harvest Bars

1¾ cups all-purpose flour
 2 teaspoons baking powder
 1 teaspoon grated orange peel
 1 teaspoon ground cinnamon
 ½ teaspoon salt
 ½ teaspoon ground nutmeg
 ¼ teaspoon ground ginger
 ¼ teaspoon ground cloves

¾ cup sugar
½ cup Mott's Natural Apple
   Sauce
½ cup solid-pack pumpkin
 1 whole egg
 1 egg white
 2 tablespoons vegetable oil
½ cup raisins

1. Preheat oven to 350°F. Spray 13×9-inch baking pan with nonstick cooking spray.

2. In small bowl, combine flour, baking powder, orange peel, cinnamon, salt, nutmeg, ginger and cloves.

3. In large bowl, combine sugar, apple sauce, pumpkin, whole egg, egg white and oil.

4. Add flour mixture to apple sauce mixture; stir until well blended. Stir in raisins. Spread batter into prepared pan.

5. Bake 25 to 30 minutes or until toothpick inserted in center comes out clean. Cool on wire rack 15 minutes; cut into 16 bars.   *Makes 16 servings*

Nutrients Per Serving:			
Calories	130	Sodium	110 mg
Total Fat	2.0 g	Cholesterol	15 mg
% of Calories From Fat	15		

Banana Cocoa Marbled Bars

½ cup uncooked rolled oats
1½ cups all-purpose flour
2 teaspoons baking powder
½ teaspoon baking soda
½ teaspoon salt
1 cup sugar
½ cup Mott's Natural Apple Sauce

1 whole egg
1 egg white
2 tablespoons vegetable oil
⅓ cup low fat buttermilk
2 tablespoons unsweetened cocoa powder
1 large ripe banana, mashed (⅔ cup)

1. Preheat oven to 350°F. Spray 9-inch square baking pan with nonstick cooking spray.

2. Place oats in food processor or blender; process until finely ground.

3. In medium bowl, combine oats, flour, baking powder, baking soda and salt.

4. In large bowl, combine sugar, apple sauce, whole egg, egg white and oil.

5. Add flour mixture to apple sauce mixture; stir until well blended. (Mixture will look dry.)

6. Remove 1 cup of batter to small bowl. Add buttermilk and cocoa; mix well.

7. Add banana to remaining batter. Mix well; spread into prepared pan.

8. Drop tablespoonfuls of cocoa batter over banana batter. Run knife through batters to marble.

9. Bake 35 minutes or until toothpick inserted in center comes out clean. Cool on wire rack 15 minutes; cut into 14 bars. *Makes 14 servings*

Nutrients Per Serving:			
Calories	160	Sodium	160 mg
Total Fat	3.0 g	Cholesterol	15 mg
% of Calories From Fat	16		

Banana Cocoa Marbled Bars

FIT FINALES

Pumpkin Apple Tart

CRUST
- 1 cup plain dry bread crumbs
- 1 cup crunchy nut-like cereal nuggets
- ½ cup sugar
- ½ teaspoon ground cinnamon
- ½ teaspoon ground nutmeg
- ¼ cup Mott's Natural Apple Sauce
- 2 tablespoons margarine, melted
- 1 egg white

FILLING
- 12 ounces evaporated skim milk
- 1½ cups solid-pack pumpkin
- ⅔ cup sugar
- ½ cup Mott's Chunky Apple Sauce
- ⅓ cup Grandma's Molasses
- 2 egg whites
- 1 whole egg
- ½ teaspoon ground ginger
- ½ teaspoon ground cinnamon
- ½ teaspoon ground nutmeg
- Frozen light nondairy whipped topping, thawed (optional)

1. Preheat oven to 375°F. Spray 9- or 10-inch springform pan with nonstick cooking spray.

2. **To prepare Crust,** in medium bowl, combine bread crumbs, cereal, ½ cup sugar, ½ teaspoon cinnamon and ½ teaspoon nutmeg.

3. Add ¼ cup apple sauce, margarine and egg white; mix until moistened. Press onto bottom of prepared pan.

4. Bake 8 minutes.

5. **To prepare Filling,** place evaporated milk in small saucepan. Cook over medium heat until milk almost boils, stirring occasionally.

continued on page 70

6. In large bowl, combine evaporated milk, pumpkin, ⅔ cup sugar, ½ cup apple sauce, molasses, 2 egg whites, whole egg, ginger, ½ teaspoon cinnamon and ½ teaspoon nutmeg. Pour into baked crust.

7. *Increase oven temperature to 400°F.* Bake 35 to 40 minutes or until center is set.

8. Cool 20 minutes on wire rack. Remove sides of pan. Spoon or pipe whipped topping onto tart, if desired. Cut into 12 slices. Refrigerate leftovers.

Makes 12 servings

Nutrients Per Serving:			
Calories	210	Sodium	170 mg
Total Fat	2.5 g	Cholesterol	20 mg
% of Calories From Fat	11		

Apple Sauce Bread Pudding

1 (16-ounce) loaf light white bread, sliced
1 cup raisins
2 teaspoons ground cinnamon
2 cups skim milk
8 egg whites

1 cup Mott's Natural Apple Sauce
½ cup firmly packed light brown sugar
1½ teaspoons vanilla extract

1. Preheat oven to 350°F. Spray 9-inch square baking pan with nonstick cooking spray.

2. Cut bread into ½-inch cubes. In large bowl, toss bread with raisins and cinnamon.

3. In medium bowl, stir together milk, egg whites, apple sauce, brown sugar and vanilla. Pour over bread cube mixture; mix well. Let stand 25 minutes. Pour mixture into prepared pan.

4. Bake 35 to 40 minutes or until knife inserted in center comes out clean. Cool 15 to 20 minutes before serving. Refrigerate leftovers.

Makes 10 servings

Nutrients Per Serving:			
Calories	210	Sodium	75 mg
Total Fat	0.5 g	Cholesterol	0 mg
% of Calories From Fat	1		

Viennese Chocolate Meringue Torte

TORTE

1¾ cups all-purpose flour
¼ cup plus 3 tablespoons
    unsweetened cocoa powder
¼ cup finely chopped walnuts
1 teaspoon baking powder
1 teaspoon ground cinnamon
½ teaspoon baking soda
½ teaspoon salt

1 cup firmly packed dark brown
    sugar
3 egg whites
1 cup Mott's Natural Apple
    Sauce
¾ cup low fat buttermilk
¾ cup dark corn syrup

MERINGUE FROSTING

1½ cups granulated sugar
 8 egg whites

¼ teaspoon salt
2 teaspoons vanilla extract

1. Preheat oven to 350°F. Spray two 9-inch round cake pans with nonstick cooking spray. Flour lightly.

2. **To prepare Torte,** in medium bowl, combine flour, cocoa, walnuts, baking powder, cinnamon, baking soda and ½ teaspoon salt.

3. In large bowl, whisk together brown sugar and 3 egg whites. Whisk in apple sauce, buttermilk and corn syrup.

4. Add flour mixture to apple sauce mixture; stir until well blended. Pour batter into prepared pans.

5. Bake 20 minutes or until toothpick inserted in centers come out clean. Cool on wire racks while preparing Meringue Frosting.

6. **To prepare Meringue Frosting,** move oven rack to center position. *Increase oven temperature to 450°F.* In top of double boiler, whisk together granulated sugar, 8 egg whites and ¼ teaspoon salt. Cook, whisking frequently, over simmering water, 3 to 4 minutes or until mixture is hot and sugar is dissolved. Remove from heat; stir in vanilla. Transfer mixture to large bowl. Beat with electric mixer at high speed 5 to 6 minutes or until thick and fluffy.

7. Place one cake layer on cookie sheet. Spread with layer of meringue. Top with second cake layer. Frost top and side with remaining meringue; swirl decoratively.

8. Bake 3 to 4 minutes or until meringue is lightly browned. Transfer to serving plate. Cut into 10 slices. Store, covered, at room temperature.

Makes 10 servings

Nutrients Per Serving:			
Calories	410	Sodium	330 mg
Total Fat	3.0 g	Cholesterol	0 mg
% of Calories From Fat	6		

Rice Pudding

1¼ cups water, divided
½ cup uncooked long-grain rice
2 cups evaporated skim milk
½ cup granulated sugar
½ cup raisins
½ cup Mott's Natural Apple
    Sauce

3 tablespoons cornstarch
1 teaspoon vanilla extract
Brown sugar or nutmeg
    (optional)
Fresh raspberries (optional)
Orange peel strips (optional)

1. In medium saucepan, bring 1 cup water to a boil. Add rice. Reduce heat to low and simmer, covered, 20 minutes or until rice is tender and water is absorbed.

2. Add milk, granulated sugar, raisins and apple sauce. Bring to a boil. Reduce heat to low and simmer for 3 minutes, stirring occasionally.

3. Combine cornstarch and remaining ¼ cup water in small bowl. Stir into rice mixture. Simmer about 20 minutes or until mixture thickens, stirring occasionally. Remove from heat; stir in vanilla. Cool 15 to 20 minutes before serving. Sprinkle each serving with brown sugar or nutmeg and garnish with raspberries and orange peel, if desired. Refrigerate leftovers.

Makes 8 servings

Nutrients Per Serving:			
Calories	190	Sodium	75 mg
Total Fat	0.5 g	Cholesterol	2 mg
% of Calories From Fat	1		

Lots O'Apple Pizza

2 cups Mott's Natural Apple
   Sauce
1 teaspoon vanilla extract
¾ teaspoon active dry yeast
½ teaspoon granulated sugar
½ cup plus 1 tablespoon warm
   water (105°-115°F)

1¼ cups all-purpose flour
½ teaspoon salt
⅔ cup raisins
2 cups unpeeled, thinly sliced
   tart apples (about 2 medium)
   Additional raisins (optional)
2 tablespoons powdered sugar

1. In medium saucepan, combine apple sauce and vanilla. Cook over medium heat, stirring occasionally, until reduced by half.

2. In small bowl, sprinkle yeast and granulated sugar over warm water; stir until yeast dissolves. Let stand 5 minutes or until mixture is bubbly.

3. In medium bowl, combine flour and salt. Make well in center of mixture.

4. Pour yeast mixture into flour mixture; stir until soft dough forms. Let rise 5 minutes. Turn out dough onto floured surface; flatten slightly. Knead 5 to 10 minutes or until smooth and elastic. Shape dough into ball; place dough in large bowl sprayed with nonstick cooking spray. Turn dough over so that top is greased. Cover with towel; let rise in warm place 45 minutes to 1 hour or until doubled in bulk.

5. Punch down dough; let rise about 30 minutes in warm place or until doubled in bulk.

6. Preheat oven to 450°F. Spray 12-inch pizza pan with nonstick cooking spray.

7. Spread dough or roll with lightly floured rolling pin into 12-inch circle. Place in prepared pan. Spread half of apple sauce mixture over dough to within ½ inch of edge. Sprinkle with ⅔ cup raisins. Arrange apple slices over pizza, covering raisins. Spread remaining apple sauce mixture over apple slices.

8. Bake 15 to 20 minutes or until edge of crust is lightly browned. Cool completely on wire rack. Garnish with additional raisins, if desired. Sprinkle with powdered sugar. Cut into 12 wedges. *Makes 12 servings*

Note: Substitute prepared pizza dough for homemade dough, if desired.

Nutrients Per Serving:			
Calories	110	Sodium	90 mg
Total Fat	0.5 g	Cholesterol	0 mg
% of Calories From Fat	2		

Lots O'Apple Pizza

Fudge Sundae Pudding

1 cup all-purpose flour
⅔ cup plus ¼ cup granulated
   sugar, divided
4 tablespoons unsweetened
   cocoa powder, divided
2 teaspoons baking powder
½ teaspoon salt
½ cup skim milk
1 teaspoon vanilla extract

½ cup firmly packed light brown
   sugar
1 cup water
1 cup Mott's Natural Apple
   Sauce
Frozen low fat vanilla yogurt
   or frozen light nondairy
   whipped topping, thawed
   (optional)

1. Preheat oven to 350°F. Spray 8-inch square baking pan with nonstick cooking spray.

2. In medium bowl, combine flour, ⅔ cup granulated sugar, 2 tablespoons cocoa, baking powder and salt. Add milk and vanilla; mix well. Spread batter into prepared pan.

3. In small bowl, combine brown sugar, remaining ¼ cup granulated sugar and 2 tablespoons cocoa. Sprinkle evenly over batter.

4. Combine water and apple sauce in small saucepan. Bring to a boil over high heat. Pour over batter. *Do not stir.*

5. Bake 35 to 40 minutes or until center is almost set. Serve immediately with frozen yogurt or whipped topping, if desired. *Makes 10 servings*

Nutrients Per Serving:			
Calories	180	Sodium	170 mg
Total Fat	0.5 g	Cholesterol	0 mg
% of Calories From Fat	2		

Apple Clafouti

2 jars (23 ounces each) Mott's
    Chunky Apple Sauce
⅔ cup raisins
1 teaspoon ground cinnamon
1 cup all-purpose flour
1 teaspoon baking powder
½ teaspoon salt
3 egg whites
¼ cup low fat buttermilk
¼ cup honey
Powdered sugar

1. Preheat oven to 400°F. Spray two 9-inch glass pie plates with nonstick cooking spray.

2. In large bowl, combine apple sauce, raisins and cinnamon.

3. In small bowl, combine flour, baking powder and salt.

4. In medium bowl, whisk together egg whites, buttermilk and honey until slightly frothy.

5. Add flour mixture to egg white mixture; whisk until well blended. Pour ½ cup batter into each prepared pie plate.

6. Bake 4 to 5 minutes or until lightly browned. Pour half of apple sauce mixture over each baked layer. Spoon remaining batter over apple sauce mixture; spread evenly.

7. *Reduce oven temperature to 350°F.* Bake 15 to 20 minutes or until tops are puffy and lightly browned.

8. Cool completely on wire racks; sprinkle tops with powdered sugar. Slice each dessert into 6 wedges. Refrigerate leftovers.   *Makes 12 servings*

Nutrients Per Serving:			
Calories	180	Sodium	135 mg
Total Fat	0.5 g	Cholesterol	0 mg
% of Calories From Fat	1		

Baked Apple Crisp

8 cups unpeeled, thinly sliced apples (about 8 medium)
2 tablespoons granulated sugar
1½ tablespoons lemon juice
4 teaspoons ground cinnamon, divided
1½ cups Mott's Natural Apple Sauce
1 cup uncooked rolled oats
½ cup firmly packed light brown sugar
⅓ cup all-purpose flour
⅓ cup evaporated skim milk
¼ cup nonfat dry milk powder
1 cup nonfat vanilla yogurt

1. Preheat oven to 350°F. Spray 2-quart casserole dish with nonstick cooking spray.

2. In large bowl, toss apple slices with granulated sugar, lemon juice and 2 teaspoons cinnamon. Spoon into prepared dish. Spread apple sauce evenly over apple mixture.

3. In medium bowl, combine oats, brown sugar, flour, evaporated milk, dry milk powder and remaining 2 teaspoons cinnamon. Spread over apple sauce.

4. Bake 35 to 40 minutes or until lightly browned and bubbly. Cool slightly; serve warm. Top each serving with dollop of yogurt.   *Makes 12 servings*

Nutrients Per Serving:			
Calories	185	Sodium	35 mg
Total Fat	1.5 g	Cholesterol	0 mg
% of Calories From Fat	6		

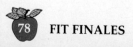

Fudge Brownie Sundaes

1 cup all-purpose flour
¾ cup granulated sugar
½ cup unsweetened cocoa
  powder, divided
2 teaspoons baking powder
½ teaspoon salt
½ cup skim milk
¼ cup Mott's Natural Apple
  Sauce

1 teaspoon vanilla extract
1¾ cups hot water
¾ cup firmly packed light brown
  sugar
½ gallon frozen nonfat vanilla
  yogurt
Maraschino cherries (optional)

1. Preheat oven to 350°F. Spray 8-inch square baking pan with nonstick cooking spray.

2. In large bowl, combine flour, granulated sugar, ¼ cup cocoa, baking powder and salt. Add milk, apple sauce and vanilla; stir until well blended. Pour batter into prepared pan.

3. In medium bowl, combine hot water, brown sugar and remaining ¼ cup cocoa. Pour over batter. *Do not stir.*

4. Bake 40 minutes or until center is almost set. Cool completely on wire rack. Cut into 12 bars. Top each bar with ½-cup scoop of frozen yogurt; spoon sauce from bottom of pan over yogurt. Garnish with cherry, if desired.

Makes 12 servings

Nutrients Per Serving:			
Calories	300	Sodium	200 mg
Total Fat	3.0 g	Cholesterol	5 mg
% of Calories From Fat	9		

Fudge Brownie Sundae

Apple Sauce Pecan Waffle Dessert

2 cups all-purpose flour
1 tablespoon baking powder
1 cup Mott's Natural Apple
    Sauce
½ cup low fat plain yogurt
¼ cup 2% milk
¼ cup firmly packed light brown
    sugar
2 tablespoons honey
1 tablespoon ground cinnamon

1 tablespoon lemon juice
¼ teaspoon ground nutmeg
4 egg whites
¼ cup finely chopped pecans
Frozen low fat vanilla yogurt
    (optional)
Additional Mott's Natural
    Apple Sauce (optional)
Fresh raspberries (optional)

1. In small bowl, sift together flour and baking powder.

2. In large bowl, combine 1 cup apple sauce, yogurt, milk, brown sugar, honey, cinnamon, lemon juice and nutmeg.

3. In medium bowl, beat egg whites with electric mixer at high speed until soft peaks form.

4. Fold egg whites and flour mixture alternately into apple sauce mixture, beginning with egg whites, until well blended. Fold in pecans.

5. Spray waffle iron with nonstick cooking spray. For every two waffles, pour ½ cup batter into hot waffle iron. Spread with knife to cover waffle iron. Close lid and bake until steaming stops.* Top each waffle with scoop of frozen yogurt, additional apple sauce and raspberries, if desired.

Makes 3 cups batter; 12 waffles

*Check the manufacturer's directions for recommended amount of baking time.

Nutrients Per Serving (1 waffle):			
Calories	140	Sodium	95 mg
Total Fat	2.0 g	Cholesterol	0 mg
% of Calories From Fat	14		

Apple Sauce Pecan Waffle Dessert

Raspberry-Apple Chiffon Torte

CRUST
- 4 slices light wheat bread, toasted
- 1 cup crunchy nut-like cereal nuggets
- 2 tablespoons frozen unsweetened apple juice concentrate, thawed
- 1 egg white
- ½ teaspoon ground nutmeg

CHIFFON
- 1 (0.3-ounce) package sugar-free raspberry gelatin
- 1 cup boiling water
- 1 cup Mott's Natural Apple Sauce
- 1 (10-ounce) package lightly sweetened frozen whole raspberries
- ½ cup sugar
- ¼ cup water
- ½ teaspoon grated lemon peel
- ½ cup evaporated skim milk, well chilled
- 1 teaspoon vanilla extract
- 2 kiwi fruit, peeled and thinly sliced
- ½ pint fresh raspberries or strawberries

1. Preheat oven to 375°F. Spray 10-inch glass pie plate with nonstick cooking spray.

2. **To prepare Crust,** in food processor or blender, process bread until fine crumbs form.

3. In medium bowl, combine bread crumbs, cereal, juice concentrate, egg white and nutmeg. Press mixture onto bottom and up side of prepared pie plate.

4. Bake 8 minutes. Cool completely on wire rack.

5. **To prepare Chiffon,** place gelatin in medium bowl. Add 1 cup boiling water; stir two minutes until gelatin is completely dissolved. Add apple sauce. Place in refrigerator until mixture mounds slightly when dropped from spoon. (For quicker set, place apple sauce mixture over large bowl filled with ice water.)

6. Combine frozen berries, sugar, ¼ cup water and lemon peel in medium saucepan. Bring to a boil over high heat. Reduce heat to low; simmer 5 to 10 minutes, stirring occasionally. Remove from heat; cool 10 minutes. Place in food processor or blender; process until smooth. Transfer to large bowl.

7. In medium bowl, beat evaporated skim milk with electric mixer at high speed until soft peaks form. Add vanilla; beat 1 minute.

8. Fold chilled gelatin mixture into berry mixture. Fold in whipped milk mixture. Spoon into cooled crust. Refrigerate at least 4 hours or overnight before serving. Top torte with kiwi fruit and fresh raspberries. Cut into 8 slices. Refrigerate leftovers. *Makes 8 servings*

Strawberry-Apple Chiffon Torte: Substitute unsweetened whole frozen strawberries for frozen raspberries and sugar-free strawberry gelatin for raspberry gelatin.

Nutrients Per Serving:			
Calories	200	Sodium	125 mg
Total Fat	0.5 g	Cholesterol	0 mg
% of Calories From Fat	2		

Apple-Lemon Sherbet

1 (16-ounce) jar Mott's Apple Sauce
½ cup frozen apple juice concentrate, thawed
¼ cup lemon juice
1 egg white*

1. In food processor or blender, process apple sauce until smooth. Add juice concentrate, lemon juice and egg white; process until frothy.

2. Pour into ice cream maker freezer container; freeze according to manufacturer's directions. Or, pour into 8- or 9-inch square pan. Cover; freeze about 2 hours or until almost firm. Transfer to food processor or blender; process until smooth. *Makes 8 servings*

*Use clean, uncracked egg.

Nutrients Per Serving:			
Calories	80	Sodium	10 mg
Total Fat	0.5 g	Cholesterol	0 mg
% of Calories From Fat	6		

SAVORY CREATIONS

Apple Stuffing

1 cup finely chopped onion
½ cup finely chopped celery
½ cup unpeeled, finely chopped apple
1½ cups Mott's Natural Apple Sauce

1 (8-ounce) package stuffing mix (original or cornbread)
1 cup defatted* chicken broth
1½ teaspoons dried thyme leaves
1 teaspoon ground sage
½ teaspoon salt
½ teaspoon black pepper

1. Spray medium nonstick skillet with nonstick cooking spray. Heat over medium heat until hot. Add onion and celery; cook and stir about 5 minutes or until transparent. Add apple; cook and stir about 3 minutes or until golden. Transfer to large bowl. Stir in remaining ingredients.

2. Loosely stuff chicken or turkey just before roasting or place stuffing in greased 8-inch square baking pan. Cover; bake in preheated 350°F oven 20 to 25 minutes or until hot. Refrigerate leftovers.   *Makes 8 servings*

*To defat chicken broth, chill canned broth thoroughly. Use can opener to punch two holes in top of can. Quickly pour out the contents of the can into bowl. Most of the fat will remain in the can and the remaining broth is "defatted."

Note: Cooked stuffing can also be used to fill centers of cooked acorn squash.

Nutrients Per Serving:			
Calories	150	Sodium	620 mg
Total Fat	1.5 g	Cholesterol	0 mg
% of Calories From Fat	8		

Apple Stuffing

Butternut Squash Soup

1 cup finely chopped onions	½ teaspoon salt
1 (3-pound) butternut squash, peeled and cubed	¼ teaspoon ground white pepper
4 cups defatted* chicken broth	¼ teaspoon ground nutmeg
1½ cups Mott's Natural Apple Sauce	¼ teaspoon ground cloves
	¼ teaspoon curry powder
	¼ teaspoon ground coriander

1. Spray large saucepan or Dutch oven with nonstick cooking spray; heat over medium heat until hot. Add onions; cook and stir about 5 minutes or until transparent.

2. Add squash, chicken broth, apple sauce, salt, pepper, nutmeg, cloves, curry powder and coriander. Increase heat to high; bring mixture to a boil. Cover; reduce heat to low. Simmer 10 to 15 minutes or until squash is fork-tender, stirring occasionally.

3. In food processor or blender, process soup in small batches until smooth. Return soup to saucepan. Cook over low heat 5 minutes or until hot, stirring occasionally. Refrigerate leftovers. *Makes 8 servings*

Microwave Directions:

1. In large microwave-safe bowl, combine onions, squash, chicken broth, apple sauce, salt, pepper, nutmeg, cloves, curry powder and coriander. Cover; cook at HIGH (100% power) 15 minutes or until squash is fork-tender, stirring once.

2. In food processor or blender, process soup in small batches until smooth. Return soup to bowl. Cover; cook at HIGH 3 minutes or until hot. Refrigerate leftovers.

*To defat chicken broth, chill canned broth thoroughly. Use can opener to punch two holes in top of can. Quickly pour out the contents of the can into bowl. Most of the fat will remain in the can and the remaining broth is "defatted."

Nutrients Per Serving:			
Calories	120	Sodium	530 mg
Total Fat	1.0 g	Cholesterol	0 mg
% of Calories From Fat	6		

Apple Burgers

1 pound ground turkey breast
1 (16-ounce) jar Mott's Apple
  Sauce, divided
2 tablespoons finely chopped
  onion

2 tablespoons finely chopped
  red or green bell pepper
¾ teaspoon salt
⅛ teaspoon ground white pepper
6 toasted buns

1. Spray broiler pan with nonstick cooking spray.

2. In large bowl, combine turkey, ½ cup apple sauce, onion, bell pepper, salt and white pepper; mix lightly. Shape mixture into 6 uniform patties. Arrange on prepared broiler pan.

3. Broil, 4 inches from heat, 5 minutes on each side or until lightly browned and no longer pink in center. Top each burger with remaining apple sauce; serve on buns. Refrigerate leftovers. *Makes 6 servings*

Nutrients Per Serving:			
Calories	300	Sodium	620 mg
Total Fat	2.0 g	Cholesterol	50 mg
% of Calories From Fat	4		

Curried Apple Onion Dip

1 (24-ounce) jar Mott's Apple
  Sauce
1 envelope (1.2-ounce package)
  onion soup mix

¼ cup plain low fat yogurt or
  low fat sour cream
1 tablespoon curry powder

1. In medium bowl, combine apple sauce, onion soup mix, yogurt and curry powder.

2. Cover; refrigerate 1 hour before serving. Serve with assorted sliced fresh vegetables. Store, covered, in refrigerator. *Makes 26 servings*

Nutrients Per Serving (2 tablespoons):			
Calories	25	Sodium	110 mg
Total Fat	0 g	Cholesterol	0 mg
% of Calories From Fat	5		

Apple-Potato Pancakes

1¼ cups unpeeled, finely chopped
    apples
  1 cup peeled, grated potatoes
  ½ cup Mott's Natural Apple
    Sauce
  ½ cup all-purpose flour

2 egg whites
1 teaspoon salt
  Additional Mott's Natural
    Apple Sauce or apple slices
    (optional)

1. Preheat oven to 475°F. Spray cookie sheet with nonstick cooking spray.

2. In medium bowl, combine apples, potatoes, ½ cup apple sauce, flour, egg whites and salt.

3. Spray large nonstick skillet with nonstick cooking spray; heat over medium heat until hot. Drop rounded tablespoonfuls of batter 2 inches apart into skillet. Cook 2 to 3 minutes on each side or until lightly browned. Place pancakes on prepared cookie sheet.

4. Bake 10 to 15 minutes or until crisp. Serve with additional apple sauce or apple slices, if desired. Refrigerate leftovers. *Makes 12 servings*

Nutrients Per Serving (1 pancake):			
Calories	60	Sodium	190 mg
Total Fat	0 g	Cholesterol	0 mg
% of Calories From Fat	2		

Apple-Potato Pancakes

Ginger Apple Chicken

4 boneless skinless chicken
   breast halves (1 pound)
1 (16-ounce) jar Mott's Apple
   Sauce

¼ cup apple-cider vinegar or
   white vinegar
2 tablespoons soy sauce
1 tablespoon grated fresh ginger
1 tablespoon honey

1. Pound chicken breasts with meat mallet to ½-inch thickness. Place in single layer in large shallow glass dish.

2. In medium bowl, combine apple sauce, vinegar, soy sauce, ginger and honey. Reserve 1 cup apple sauce mixture. Pour remaining apple sauce mixture over chicken; turn to coat both sides. Cover; marinate in refrigerator at least 20 minutes or overnight.

3. Drain chicken; discard marinade from dish.

4. Broil chicken, on foil-lined baking sheet, 4 inches from heat, 10 minutes or until chicken is no longer pink in center, turning halfway through cooking time. Or, grill chicken, on covered grill over medium-hot coals, 10 minutes or until chicken is no longer pink in center, turning halfway through cooking time. Serve with reserved apple sauce mixture, warmed or at room temperature. Refrigerate leftovers. *Makes 4 servings*

Nutrients Per Serving:			
Calories	240	Sodium	600 mg
Total Fat	1.5 g	Cholesterol	70 mg
% of Calories From Fat	6		

Orchard BBQ Sauce

2 cloves garlic, minced
1 (24-ounce) jar Mott's Apple
   Sauce
½ cup apple-cider vinegar
½ cup tomato paste

¼ cup Grandma's Molasses
¼ cup soy sauce
1 teaspoon paprika
¼ to ½ teaspoon ground red
   pepper

1. Spray medium nonstick saucepan with nonstick cooking spray; heat over medium heat until hot. Add garlic. Cook and stir 2 to 3 minutes; do not brown.

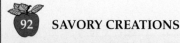

2. Add apple sauce, vinegar, tomato paste, molasses, soy sauce, paprika and ground red pepper; stir until blended. Increase heat to high; bring mixture to a boil. Cover; reduce heat to low. Simmer 10 minutes, stirring occasionally.

3. Store up to 2 weeks in tightly sealed container in refrigerator.

Makes 16 servings

Nutrients Per Serving (2 tablespoons):			
Calories	30	Sodium	160 mg
Total Fat	0 g	Cholesterol	0 mg
% of Calories From Fat	3		

Saucy Potato Salad

¼ cup chopped onion
1 (16-ounce) jar Mott's Apple Sauce
⅓ cup vinegar
¼ cup thinly sliced celery
1 tablespoon Dijon-style mustard *or* ½ teaspoon dry mustard

8 medium red-skinned potatoes (about 3 pounds), peeled, cooked and sliced
¾ cup chopped dill pickle
Salt (optional)
Pepper (optional)

1. Spray large nonstick saucepan with nonstick cooking spray; heat over medium heat until hot. Add onion; cook and stir about 3 minutes or until transparent.

2. Stir in apple sauce, vinegar, celery and mustard. Increase heat to high; bring mixture to a boil, stirring occasionally.

3. Place potatoes in large bowl; add pickle. Pour hot apple sauce mixture over potato mixture; toss until well coated. Add salt and pepper, if desired. Serve immediately or cover and refrigerate until serving. Refrigerate leftovers.

Makes 8 servings

Nutrients Per Serving:			
Calories	180	Sodium	90 mg
Total Fat	0.5 g	Cholesterol	0 mg
% of Calories From Fat	2		

INDEX

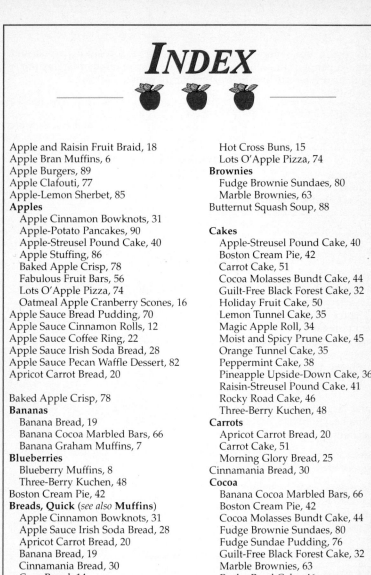

Apple and Raisin Fruit Braid, 18
Apple Bran Muffins, 6
Apple Burgers, 89
Apple Clafouti, 77
Apple-Lemon Sherbet, 85
Apples
  Apple Cinnamon Bowknots, 31
  Apple-Potato Pancakes, 90
  Apple-Streusel Pound Cake, 40
  Apple Stuffing, 86
  Baked Apple Crisp, 78
  Fabulous Fruit Bars, 56
  Lots O'Apple Pizza, 74
  Oatmeal Apple Cranberry Scones, 16
Apple Sauce Bread Pudding, 70
Apple Sauce Cinnamon Rolls, 12
Apple Sauce Coffee Ring, 22
Apple Sauce Irish Soda Bread, 28
Apple Sauce Pecan Waffle Dessert, 82
Apricot Carrot Bread, 20

Baked Apple Crisp, 78
Bananas
  Banana Bread, 19
  Banana Cocoa Marbled Bars, 66
  Banana Graham Muffins, 7
Blueberries
  Blueberry Muffins, 8
  Three-Berry Kuchen, 48
Boston Cream Pie, 42
Breads, Quick (*see also* **Muffins**)
  Apple Cinnamon Bowknots, 31
  Apple Sauce Irish Soda Bread, 28
  Apricot Carrot Bread, 20
  Banana Bread, 19
  Cinnamania Bread, 30
  Corn Bread, 14
  Lemon Poppy Seed Tea Loaf, 26
  Morning Glory Bread, 25
  Oatmeal Apple Cranberry Scones, 16
  Zucchini and Date Tea Loaf, 24
Breads, Yeast
  Apple and Raisin Fruit Braid, 18
  Apple Sauce Cinnamon Rolls, 12
  Apple Sauce Coffee Ring, 22
  Hot Cross Buns, 15
  Lots O'Apple Pizza, 74
Brownies
  Fudge Brownie Sundaes, 80
  Marble Brownies, 63
Butternut Squash Soup, 88

Cakes
  Apple-Streusel Pound Cake, 40
  Boston Cream Pie, 42
  Carrot Cake, 51
  Cocoa Molasses Bundt Cake, 44
  Guilt-Free Black Forest Cake, 32
  Holiday Fruit Cake, 50
  Lemon Tunnel Cake, 35
  Magic Apple Roll, 34
  Moist and Spicy Prune Cake, 45
  Orange Tunnel Cake, 35
  Peppermint Cake, 38
  Pineapple Upside-Down Cake, 36
  Raisin-Streusel Pound Cake, 41
  Rocky Road Cake, 46
  Three-Berry Kuchen, 48
Carrots
  Apricot Carrot Bread, 20
  Carrot Cake, 51
  Morning Glory Bread, 25
Cinnamania Bread, 30
Cocoa
  Banana Cocoa Marbled Bars, 66
  Boston Cream Pie, 42
  Cocoa Molasses Bundt Cake, 44
  Fudge Brownie Sundaes, 80
  Fudge Sundae Pudding, 76
  Guilt-Free Black Forest Cake, 32
  Marble Brownies, 63
  Rocky Road Cake, 46
  Tri-Layer Chocolate Oatmeal Bars, 60
  Viennese Chocolate Meringue Torte, 71
Cookies, Bar (*see also* **Brownies**)
  Apple Oatmeal Snack Bars, 58
  Banana Cocoa Marbled Bars, 66
  Fabulous Fruit Bars, 56
  Lemon Bars, 55

Pumpkin Harvest Bars, 64
Tri-Layer Chocolate Oatmeal Bars, 60
Cookies, Drop
Gingersnaps, 52
Jam Thumbprint Gems, 62
Oatmeal Cookies, 54
Corn Bread, 14
Cranberries
Fabulous Fruit Bars, 56
Oatmeal Apple Cranberry Scones, 16
Curried Apple Onion Dip, 89

Desserts (*see also* **Puddings**, **Tarts**, **Tortes**)
Apple Clafouti, 77
Apple-Lemon Sherbet, 85
Apple Sauce Pecan Waffle Dessert, 82
Baked Apple Crisp, 78
Fudge Brownie Sundaes, 80
Lots O'Apple Pizza, 74

Fabulous Fruit Bars, 56
Fudge Brownie Sundaes, 80
Fudge Sundae Pudding, 76

Ginger Apple Chicken, 92
Gingersnaps, 52
Guilt-Free Black Forest Cake, 32

Heavenly Lemon Muffins, 10
Heavenly Strawberry Muffins, 10
Holiday Fruit Cake, 50
Hot Cross Buns, 15

Jam Thumbprint Gems, 62

Lemon
Apple-Lemon Sherbet, 85
Heavenly Lemon Muffins, 10
Lemon Bars, 55
Lemon Poppy Seed Tea Loaf, 26
Lemon Tunnel Cake, 35
Lots O'Apple Pizza, 74

Magic Apple Roll, 34
Main Dishes
Apple Burgers, 89
Ginger Apple Chicken, 92
Marble Brownies, 63
Moist and Spicy Prune Cake, 45
Morning Glory Bread, 25

Muffins
Apple Bran Muffins, 6
Banana Graham Muffins, 7
Blueberry Muffins, 8
Heavenly Lemon Muffins, 10
Heavenly Strawberry Muffins, 10
Peach Gingerbread Muffins, 4

Oatmeal Apple Cranberry Scones, 16
Oatmeal Cookies, 54
Orange Tunnel Cake, 35
Orchard BBQ Sauce, 92

Peach Gingerbread Muffins, 4
Peppermint Cake, 38
Pineapple
Holiday Fruit Cake, 50
Morning Glory Bread, 25
Pineapple Upside-Down Cake, 36
Puddings
Apple Sauce Bread Pudding, 70
Fudge Sundae Pudding, 76
Rice Pudding, 72
Pumpkin Apple Tart, 68
Pumpkin Harvest Bars, 64

Raisin-Streusel Pound Cake, 41
Raspberries
Raspberry-Apple Chiffon Torte, 84
Three-Berry Kuchen, 48
Rice Pudding, 72
Rocky Road Cake, 46

Saucy Potato Salad, 93
Side Dishes
Apple-Potato Pancakes, 90
Apple Stuffing, 86
Butternut Squash Soup, 88
Saucy Potato Salad, 93
Strawberry-Apple Chiffon Torte, 85

Tarts; Pumpkin Apple Tart, 68
Three-Berry Kuchen, 48
Tortes
Raspberry-Apple Chiffon Torte, 84
Strawberry-Apple Chiffon Torte, 85
Viennese Chocolate Meringue Torte, 71
Tri-Layer Chocolate Oatmeal Bars, 60

Viennese Chocolate Meringue Torte, 71

Zucchini and Date Tea Loaf, 24

INDEX 95

METRIC CONVERSION CHART

VOLUME MEASUREMENTS (dry)

⅛ teaspoon = 0.5 mL
¼ teaspoon = 1 mL
½ teaspoon = 2 mL
¾ teaspoon = 4 mL
1 teaspoon = 5 mL
1 tablespoon = 15 mL
2 tablespoons = 30 mL
¼ cup = 60 mL
⅓ cup = 75 mL
½ cup = 125 mL
⅔ cup = 150 mL
¼ cup = 175 mL
1 cup = 250 mL
2 cups = 1 pint = 500 mL
3 cups = 750 mL
4 cups = 1 quart = 1 L

VOLUME MEASUREMENTS (fluid)

1 fluid ounce (2 tablespoons) = 30 mL
4 fluid ounces (½ cup) = 125 mL
8 fluid ounces (1 cup) = 250 mL
12 fluid ounces (1½ cups) = 375 mL
16 fluid ounces (2 cups) = 500 mL

WEIGHTS (mass)

½ ounce = 15 g
1 ounce = 30 g
3 ounces = 90 g
4 ounces = 120 g
8 ounces = 225 g
10 ounces = 285 g
12 ounces = 360 g
16 ounces = 1 pound = 450 g

DIMENSIONS

1/16 inch = 2 mm
⅛ inch = 3 mm
¼ inch = 6 mm
½ inch = 1.5 cm
¾ inch = 2 cm
1 inch = 2.5 cm

OVEN TEMPERATURES

250°F = 120°C
275°F = 140°C
300°F = 150°C
325°F = 160°C
350°F = 180°C
375°F = 190°C
400°F = 200°C
425°F = 220°C
450°F = 230°C

BAKING PAN SIZES

Utensil	Size in Inches/ Quarts	Metric Volume	Size in Centimeters
Baking or Cake Pan (square or rectangular)	8×8×2	2 L	20×20×5
	9×9×2	2.5 L	22×22×5
	12×8×2	3 L	30×20×5
	13×9×2	3.5 L	33×23×5
Loaf Pan	8×4×3	1.5 L	20×10×7
	9×5×3	2 L	23×13×7
Round Layer Cake Pan	8 × 1½	1.2 L	20×4
	9 × 1½	1.5 L	23×4
Pie Plate	8 × 1¼	750 mL	20×3
	9 × 1¼	1 L	23×3
Baking Dish or Casserole	1 quart	1 L	—
	1½ quart	1.5 L	—
	2 quart	2 L	—